LABORGISTICS®

Dominique Roux

LABORGISTICS®

A New Strategy for Management

Foreword by Jack R. Wentworth

ECONOMICA

49, rue Héricart, 75015 Paris

CONTENTS

FOREWORD

Today's managers are facing an increasing magnitude of pressures for change. Over a century ago, we endured the Industrial Revolution that changed many countries, and especially the United States, from an agrarian society to an industrial society. Today, we are under the same level of pressure to change from a domestic economy to a global economy which, in turn, is causing societal as well as political changes. Arguably, the most significant issue facing business management as global competition increases is the concept referred to as *outsourcing*.

Dominique Roux, noted French business scholar, author and business consultant, recognized the growing importance of this hitherto unseen phenomenon he refers to as *globalization*. This book traces the environmental changes that generated globalization and its management consequences. Of particular importance in the United States is the issue of outsourcing in its different forms, which, in addition to being an economic issue, is becoming a political issue. Outsourcing is increasing dramatically and needs to be better understood and placed in some kind of conceptual structure – a logical and practical framework. Roux does just that.

Roux does this by giving outsourcing the theoretical base that it needs and deserves. This book is an excellent blend of theory and practice and helps us understand the reasons for what we see happening today. If management better understands outsourcing, it will be less of a threat; but rather, will open new opportunities to meet ever increasing global competition. In other words, if we truly understand the evolution of outsourcing, we are in a better position to capitalize on a phenomenon that was inevitable.

In the first two chapters, Roux lays the groundwork for what he refers to as worldwide *hypercompetition*. He helps the reader understand that this is not a condition brought about by large business firms, but by decisions made by governments following World War II. Hence, these decisions were probably inevitable as we examine history and its corresponding economic theory that led us to that point in time.

Clearly, two world wars made it obvious that a country would not live within its own borders. At the same time, other critical factors included dramatic changes in technology, communications, transportation and logistics. Roux points out that the result is an environment of hypercompetition within which firms must compete. This resulted in new pressures on management of these firms. The systematic striving for efficiency becomes a requirement for survival by maintaining a competitive edge. In turn, this leads to the need for new management tools, techniques and approaches.

Roux provides a clear and logical base for these developments and offers new management approaches to achieve greater efficiency and more flexibility as well as greater cost effectiveness. These approaches include greater management attention to such issues as a company's core business (competencies), supply-chain management, subcontracting, outsourcing, and even the development of a network of companies.

This background provides a more meaningful understanding of what is happening in a very competitive global economic environment and why it is happening. This understanding becomes even more important as Roux identifies, defines and compares these approaches and places them in a strong strategic framework.

All of this leads to the major theme of the book and a whole new level of strategy for the business firm that must compete in this dramatically changing environment. For the past few years, I have had the privilege of serving with Dominique Roux on the advisory board of a firm that is now named International Outsourcing Services (IOS). We have had the unusual advantage of witnessing new strategies develop in this competitive environment, not only as IOS, but within firms with whom IOS does business. Roux felt that change was happening so rapidly that there was a need to examine these changes in the context of management theory to see why it was happening and evaluate the next developments. Roux saw the value of a new concept of management that was developing and wanted to share it through a book. He also saw the need for bringing together some of the management theory that was relevant. I agreed to do some editing for the English version and write this foreword.

What we saw happening was that the supply-chain management was becoming critically important in this changing global environment. It was becoming a vital part of the firm's overall competitive strategy. For example, most successful firms clearly recognize the need for strategic *marketing* on the "downstream" side of the firm. Now, the need for strategic *procurement* on the "upstream" side of the firm takes on greater importance.

As IOS looked at these management needs, it called for a new level of commitment to a strategy that went beyond subcontracting or contract manufacturing or outsourcing and needed its own identification. That's when the term *Laborgistics*® was created.

It would be very easy to pass this off as a new management buzzword or just a new name for old practices. However, I feel (and, obviously, so does Roux) it is much more than that – it is a strategic way of thinking and conceptualizing. It brings the *market* into the upstream side of things to a much greater extent. To a much greater degree, strategic procurement becomes more significant and requires tighter integration with strategic marketing on the downstream. As Roux points out, it also has obvious implications to the organization structure of the firm. It is this kind of corporate thinking that is needed, perhaps required, as we move into an increasingly competitive global environment.

Perhaps it would be helpful to understand some important but subtle distinctions between simple *outsourcing* and *Laborgistics*®:

– Outsourcing tends to focus on cost cutting – Laborgistics® focuses on generating new revenue as well as cutting costs to identify and/or take advantage of new market opportunities.

– Simple outsourcing tends to have a survivor focus – Laborgistics® has a long-term, strategic focus.

– Regular outsourcing infers "working cheaper" – Laborgistics® infers "working smarter."

– Outsourcing is often with an individual vendor – Laborgistics® is often involved with multiple vendors or, as Roux calls it, a "network of partners."

– Outsourcing may send some jobs overseas – Laborgistics® may send some jobs overseas, but it may also create new strategic jobs both in the domestic country and overseas.

Roux gives much "food for thought" as to what and why we face the changes we are experiencing. It is based on both management theory and practice, but the two combined give us a better understanding of where we are and what we need to do. In a very real sense, each chapter can stand on its own, yet there is a flow of logic that results in appreciating the importance of the global competition we face. As a result, the reader comes away with knowledge of the logic and importance of Laborgistics® and how this concept might help a given business enterprise.

As a final thought, I want to call attention to the _Glossary of a few management concepts_ at the end of Chapter V. This is an excellent compilation of practical definitions of business concepts that are, and will play, vital roles in both our business and political lives. It's a good way to "get up to date" quickly.

Jack. R. Wentworth

PROLOGUE

LABORGISTICS®: A HISTORY

How a groundbreaking management system has supplanted the inherently flawed model of traditional outsourcing.

The roots of the company credited with rethinking the traditional model of global outsourcing reach back to the early days of the Information Age and worldwide competition. IOS was organized initially as a data services provider. Through corporate restructuring, global acquisitions, strategic alignments and the application of technology, the company's scope of operations dramatically increased.

By the 21st century, IOS had been shaped into an entirely new corporate entity. In the process, concurrent initiatives created inherent efficiencies and cost reductions that gave rise to a new business model for supply chain structure and outsourcing management – Laborgistics®.

IOS analysis showed that traditional outsourcing partnerships were inherently imbalanced and burdened with superfluous management structures that failed to add value to the outsourcing process. Based almost exclusively on rapid cost reduction, these relationships lacked broader, strategic underpinnings and offered little prospects for long-term viability. In their wake, failed outsourcing ventures had a destructive effect on corporate finances, employment and the economies of nations.

Laborgistics® methodology realizes long-term productivity gains and cost reduction through consolidation of management, more effective organization of global labor and more efficient supply chain structures. Unique Laborgistics® management technologies bridge a global sourcing network with worldwide production and distribution centers, all unified under the codes of international quality standards: ISO 9001, SAS 70, USFDA, HACCP, U.S. Department of Defense certifications, Homeland Security certifications and the principles of Six Sigma. With this unique structure, IOS presents a singular channel for comprehensive management of labor and supply chain, unfettered by the weaknesses of the traditional outsourcing model. Laborgistics® brings together people and technologies to provide a world of solutions for contemporary business and manufacturing.

With Laborgistics®, IOS has, in essence, created a new system of "lean management" that offers significant cost controls and supply chain enhancement to myriad companies worldwide. In practice at IOS, Laborgistics® is presented in two primary service categories: Contract Manufacturing and Data Services. This operational structure reflects the duality of the contemporary global economy and establishes clear entrées into Laborgistics® for customers in all industries, from manufacturing to financial services.

In the emerging age of global hypercompetition, the waning of the traditional outsourcing model and increasing reliance on vastly extended supply chains, Laborgistics® promises to bring a new dimension of management solutions to the complexities of worldwide manufacturing and service sector economics.

INTRODUCTION

Studying the development of human societies from Antiquity to today reveals one notable feature: the significant increase in production and exchange, at both worldwide and individual levels.

Technical progress has admittedly been one of the prerequisites for this phenomenon, and development has taken place parallel to the growth in the size and complexity of the companies that drive it forward. The result has been the gradual surfacing of new opportunities and problems, themselves leading to the emergence of methods providing specific solutions.

The need to ensure the political coherence of societies had, since time immemorial, led to the establishment of rules that, incidentally, vary greatly according to the time and place, and that govern their organization. Their nature and efficiency had also long been under consideration. Some of these rules were economic, as a corollary of the specialization of tasks within societies was that a number of their members (for example governors, administrators, members of the priesthood and soldiers) did not participate directly in productive activities, and could only subsist through duties paid on such activities, this payment having to be organized. Codification occasionally even bore on the practice of exchange, as this was considered a fundamental factor in the social process (see the Hammourabi Code, 23 BC).

However, the issues raised by the growth of merchant organizations soon proved to be profoundly different from those encountered and resolved in the political arena. The interests at stake are less fundamental, as they are more private than collective, and mostly concern the notion of property. The individual is not over-shadowed by the company to which he belongs[1]; the contract binding them is personal rather than social. Finally, the very nature of the activities pursued by these organizations leads to the emergence of highly specific technical problems, worlds apart from those arising in the operation of political systems.

Under pressure from economic developments there gradually arose a set of procedures and rules of behavior, the purpose of which is to ensure the greatest possible efficiency in the running of companies. This field came to be known as management.

Companies are by nature multi-dimensional entities due to the great diversity of facets apparent in their functioning. Company management, both as a scientific discipline and as a practice, obviously reflects this variety of aspects.

Since Fayol[2] and Taylor it has been acknowledged that it is possible to reduce this diversity to a limited number of major operational categories known as functions: accounting, financial management, marketing, human resource management, production management, planning & analysis, supervision, and now informatics. Although very different in terms of the techniques they use, these functions are in fact closely interdependent. Such links exist because the attainment of the objectives the company sets itself requires coordination of the activities. There is no sense in producing without being able to sell, or in selling without setting up a system to assess the results.

However, beyond the major technical fields falling into the management sphere, understanding and running a large concern requires a more cross-company approach. Today, it has been noted that all functions within firms undergo profound transformations under the influence of general phenomena affecting all companies.

These transformations occur within an economic environment that is itself subject to constant change. The trend is towards a reinforcement of competition and an alteration of its processes. The glo-

---

1. No one has ever considered transposing the Roman adage *Dulce et decorum est pro patria mori* ("It is sweet and fitting to die for one's fatherland") to companies, despite the fact it is still one of the foundations of modern societies' political organization.

2. H. Fayol (1841-1925) a French management thinker and F.W. Taylor (1856-1915) an American management thinker.

balization of markets, deregulation processes and the perspectives of new markets are forcing companies to be more rigorous and more dynamic in their management. The systematic striving towards efficiency is becoming a requirement for survival. To obtain, or to keep, their competitive edge, companies must not only be able to adapt to changes in the environment, but also to anticipate them, and even induce them. This is why developments emerging in the field of management are both fundamental and swift.

Thus the value chain, production methods and organization are today being debated, and even contested; new models are emerging, enabling companies to keep their positions. The outsourcing or contracting-out[1] of certain activities, which used to be considered a peripheral or occasional practice with limited scope, is now often becoming an essential part of company strategy. New concepts are being studied and new organizational methods are being adopted. A notable example of this is "Laborgistics®", which makes it possible, so long as a number of precautions are taken, to improve the performance of companies of any size, wherever they may be located, within the current context.

---

1. This process consists of cooperation among different companies with complementary potentials to develop synergy.

CHAPTER 1 :

WORLDWIDE HYPERCOMPETITION

As the 21st century begins, world economics are undergoing a major upheaval due to a phenomenon hitherto unseen in the history of humankind: globalization, which implies the opening of markets and the almost worldwide freedom of exchange.

Since Antiquity, and more particularly since the 16th century, international trade has always existed, but has been limited to specific, restricted geographical areas, for example the silk and spice routes. What is new in the current situation is that this development of commercial exchanges is almost worldwide, and its large scale has led to a massive increase in competition having a variety of effects in terms of both the price and quality of the products and manufacturing and delivery deadlines. The customer has become correspondingly demanding, thus making it necessary to adapt companies' organization, production and management methods.

A Political Objective

This globalization of economies did not originate, as is sometimes asserted, in the wish of major multinational companies to expand their influence so as to dominate the world a little more, but first and foremost in various institutional decisions mostly initiated by post-war governments. These governments advanced two arguments for their wish to break down trade barriers:

– The first was a question of economics, and was based on the various theories arguing in favor of considering international trade as a major factor in growth and the creation of wealth. Maintaining strict control over markets was no longer an issue, as such measures were widely held responsible for the Great Depression of the 1930s.

– The second was more philosophical. A great many politicians who had lived through the War and countries' tendencies to withdraw into themselves believed that this isolationist vision had been one of the major causes of the tensions and violence that devastated the world by encouraging state belligerence.

Once the hostilities were over, negotiations were started with a view to setting up the General Agreement on Tariffs and Trade (GATT), the aim of which was to reduce or gradually remove customs barriers by rejecting protectionism and implementing the principles of free exchange and payment laid down as a result of the Bretton Woods Agreement signed in 1944.

Borne along by this movement, the 1957 Treaty of Rome founded the EEC (European Economic Community), which was to become the European Union, and since then, as shown in the following table, the movement has steadily grown, continuing today – through the WTO (World Trade Organization) – to encourage the world's market to open up as much as possible.

The success of the EEC was then to encourage the founding of various free exchange areas with similar objectives in several other parts of the world, for example in North America (NAFTA) and South America (Mercosur).

It should not be forgotten that this globalization of activities and exchanges arose from the last half-century's astounding scientific and technological progress in the information and communication sectors[1], and especially in telecommunications (long-distance communication). Within companies, the basic need for information, consisting in creating links among individuals and events, has been transformed into a need for communication, meaning the exchange of information between individuals, and by extension telecommunications, thus breaking free of spatial constraints.

Another factor that has contributed to encouraging the development of increasingly world-oriented markets is the progress made in the field of transportation in all its forms (land, sea and air). Constantly improving performance and ever-falling prices have widely

---

1. Notably the invention of the transistor in 1948.

Institutional Globalization

1. The GATT set up in 1947.

2. The Treaty of Rome signed in 1957, initially bringing together 6 countries, then 9 in 1973, 10 in 1981, 12 in 1986, 15 in 1995 and soon 25 in 2004. The European Union currently has 370 million inhabitants.

3. J.F. Kennedy's presidency saw the passing of the Trade Expansion Act, in 1962, which was to serve as a basis for many international negotiations on the reduction of customs duties: the Kennedy Round (1964-1968), then the Tokyo Round (1973-1979), and finally the Uruguay Round (1986-1994), considered the founding act of globalization.

4. The World Trade Organization (WTO) was founded in 1994 following the Marrakesh Agreement, to promote exchanges on a non-discriminatory basis, to avoid local protectionist policies and to broaden the scope of the agreements to agriculture and services.

5. In 1994 came the North American Free Trade Agreement (NAFTA), signed by Canada, the United States and Mexico, and this, with 390 million inhabitants, today constitutes the world's largest free trade area.

6. 1991 saw the advent of the Mercado Común del Sur (Mercosur), initially brining together four countries: Brazil, Argentina, Uruguay and Paraguay. They were joined in 1996 by Chile and Bolivia, and the whole area has 230 million inhabitants.

7. In 2001, 8 Muslim countries (Bangladesh, Egypt, Indonesia, Iran, Malaysia, Nigeria, Pakistan and Turkey) signed the Cairo Declaration forming a group known as "D8", the aim of which is to assume common positions during negotiations with the WTO.

8. In Miami in 1994, Bill Clinton launched the project of setting up a pan-American free exchange zone (FTAA: Free Trade Area of the Americas). This should bring together 34 countries, from Alaska to Tierra del Fuego, with a total population of 800 million, and should open on January 1, 2005.

---

encouraged the increased mobility of all production factors, particularly productive capital.

This globalization, which has revolutionized the world economy, may, for example, be measured in terms of the number of international telephone calls made – a tenfold increase over the last 20 years, not included cell phones calls – or of proportion of foreign trade in countries' GNP. From 1990 to 2001 imports into France rose from 22% to 26% of the total French product, from 25% to 33% in Germany and from 11% to 15% in the United States. Exports also increased by similar percentages.

In 1985, worldwide exchanges amounted to 2,000 billion dollars among the 90 members of the WTO equivalent of the time, and today, for 143 members, they exceed 7,000 billion dollars. Generally speaking, since the Second World War, growth in international trade has been faster than growth in national production. Since 1960, in terms of volume the growth rate for international trade has been three times higher than that of production. For 2003, the provisional figures should be equivalent, since for a worldwide increase in GDP of 2.3%, exchanges are estimated at 6.2%.

Questioning Theories of International Trade

Theories of international trade based on the comparative advantages, which recommend that each country specializes in production for which it has an edge over other countries, and which have barely altered since the writings of D. Ricardo in 1817, "are now dead". They only took individual nations into account, ignoring the position and role of companies. However, it is clearly these very companies that produce and proceed with the majority of economic relations by expanding their operations internationally in three main forms: international trade, direct investment abroad and more recently network companies. This third form of expansion consists, instead of setting up subsidiaries, in developing contractual relations with different partners, most particularly in developing countries.

Company strategies determine absolute and relative costs among industries; it is not the comparative costs that dictate strategy. Since traditional theories are based on comparative advantages, they are still useful in examining issues relating to international exchanges, as they do provide certain information. However, they are being increasingly supplanted by the principle of competitive rather than comparative advantages, emphasizing the determination with which companies fight to maintain their positions. Thus international trade is regarded as a means to accumulate wealth for all the agents, from producers and customers to intermediaries. However, it should be added that this positive process is not painless for those who are not capable of attaining this famous competitive edge.

A Transformed Productive System

Not only can globalization not be reduced to a mere increase in trade, however great the volume of exchange may be, it also causes increasing interdependence among national economies, leading to a radically different productive system.

This globalization leads to new openings while at the same time increasing competition, all this leading in turn to double-faceted question of how to maintain a competitive edge in the face of new competition and how to operate on a more international level. To respond to these challenges and maintain or even increase competitiveness, all the components of a company, from organization and functioning to management methods must be reconsidered. Parallel to this, an appropriate corporate structure must be set up, and this structure must in no way hinder this quest for competitiveness by imposing quotas, customs duties or any other measures so as to protect domestic markets. Finally, the various costs of factors that differ from country to country[1] must be taken into account so as to improve given situations. This is sometimes feasible, but given the differences in development levels is often an impossible task, thus leading to delocalization or outsourcing.

The impacts of the globalization of economies and the sociological and technological transformations that have either accompanied it or resulted from it have had major repercussions on companies and the way they are managed. This caused fundamental changes in production conditions, which dramatically reduces their profitability. Some companies even went under, a notable example being PanAm, the biggest airline in the world. They had to react quickly and comprehensively.

In this new context, companies had to face new risks. This led to them increasing their productivity by reducing staffing levels considerably and changing the geographical area and conditions of their operations. Almost all companies, from the smallest to the largest, were forced to start "thinking global".

To respond to these changes in their environment, they started refocussing their core businesses or their key areas of expertise to avoid spreading themselves too thinly, outsourcing more and more tasks they had been carrying out themselves until then. Some even went as far as setting up what are known as "network companies", within which the hierarchical organization is abandoned in favor of increased independence and flexibility.

---

1. In 2003, a worker's average hourly wage was $2.30 in Mexico, $3 in India and $1.35 in China, compared with $8 in the United States, plus the variance in benefit cost.

Taking the Environment into Account

The rules of the game have been changed, the barriers that used to protect the leaders in any given sector have largely been broken down, and the limits of companies have been called into question. Companies are no longer separated from their environments, and production units are working increasingly closely with their partners. Finally, and perhaps most importantly, companies are being forced to adapt to changes in their environments by altering their production projects so as to maintain or improve their positions – in short, to stay competitive. In this new context, the winners are the fastest and the most daring. This is why new strategies had to be developed, for it is no longer enough to make the most of skills already acquired; it is vital to overcome weaknesses by acquiring new skills, and this as economically as possible.

Any analysis of company behavior must be based on consideration of internal and external environments. External factors impose constraints on a firm, and thus restrict its freedom of action. Reciprocally, however, the strategies pursued by companies aim at altering these constraints. Laborgistics® is for example one of these strategies, to be defined in Chapter IV. The relationship between a company and its environment is thus interactive.

In this respect, the traditional theories of the market adopt an extremely simplistic approach, considering that causality is a one-way street, going from the environment to the company; no retro-action is possible. The firm is subject to internal constraints by virtue of its role as producer. Otherwise, the emphasis is essentially on the competitive situation within the sector, characterized by the number of offerors. With some exceptions (monopoly or bilateral oligopoly), suppliers and customers are generally fairly dispersed. Against this backdrop, it is usually possible to define balanced values within the market that are only modified if the conditions in the environment alter exogenously.

Reality proves to be distinctly more complex for several reasons. The first is the existence of interaction between firms and their environments. It would not be going too far to state that one of the major objectives of strategy is to attempt to shift the constraints that are imposed upon companies. The second is that the environment of a company comprises other factors than those examined by market theoreticians, for example, potential entrants, interchangeable products, technological breakthroughs and of course government intervention. Finally, the way the environment is interpreted is far too simplistic. For example, characterizing the competition merely by the number of offerors is reductive.

A diagram, inspired by Porter's work[1], illustrates this. Included in the diagram are the factors habitually taken into account to characterize the position of companies in the competitive process: market structure (concentration and bars to access), intensity of competition, relations with customers and suppliers, the threat of substitute products and potential new companies entering the market. It also became clear that certain more indirect components of the company's environment needed to be included, since they may exert a crucial influence on the process and outcome of competition, but are generally not directly involved. The major factors are government intervention, financial markets and technical advances arising from other sectors of the economy.

Graphic – **Exhibit: The Company and its Environment (after Porter)**

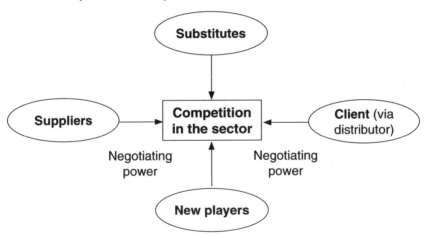

This exhibit sets out in static form the main relations between companies and their environments. This representation is convenient, but it should not be forgotten that there are widespread interactions not only between the company and its environment but also among the various factors making up this environment. The emer-

---

1. *Competitive Strategy: Techniques for Analyzing Industries and Competitors*, New York, Free Press, 1980.

gence of products that may be substituted for those available on the market may, for example, modify customer behavior, and that of backers, potential market entrants and rival firms. For the company under consideration, the adoption of a new production process may also have similar consequences.

Light should be shed on one particular problem concerning information relating to this environment and how it develops. Information is a costly product, and any given company must gather it before being able to make use of it. A useful distinction is thus to be made between the narrow environment and the broad environment. The first brings together agents whose behavior has direct and important influence on the situation of a company and may well alter this situation frequently and at short notice. The company must thus be able to develop tactics that enable it to react swiftly. Competitors on the market clearly fall into this category. The broad environment consists of agents whose behavior is more stable or in whom any change would lead to less immediate consequences on the company's situation.

Changes to the narrow environment concern, at least initially, the tactical management of the company, whereas those in the broad environment influence more strategic management. Thus the information needs regarding these two environments differ. Monitoring of changes in the narrow environment must be more detailed than for the broad environment, but in both cases, information must be gathered systematically.

As Porter has pointed out, management must take into account four forces that influence, each in its own way, the mechanisms of competition:
– the development of supplier powers;
– the threat from new players on the market;
– developments in power for distributors and customers;
– the threat from substitute products.

Globalization will thus lead to stiffer competition as a result of the sharply increasing number of competitors, of permanent benchmarking leading to considerable drops in price and of constant striving for quality and ever-tighter delivery schedules.

The World of Hypercompetition

Hypercompetition is today the new environment for firms, with the arrival *en masse* on the existing markets of new, flexible and creative companies whose success is based on very short production cycles and product life, plus constant innovation. With globalization, barriers are breaking down all over; no company can consider itself safe, nor believe that it has a niche with its name on it. All companies have had to revise their operating methods. In this age of hypercompetition, newcomers, both local and foreign, enter the market with such force that they seriously challenge – and sometimes topple – the old-guard leaders.

This has been the case, for example, for computer software and hardware manufacturers Microsoft, Intel, Dell and Compaq, who took on the giant IBM both in product design and in the production and use of factors. The same has been true in the telecommunications equipment sector, with Cisco against Lucent, Alcatel Ericsson and Nortel.

In this new context, the competition rapidly changes pace or location, putting rivals into a much greater state of uncertainty than in the past. These changes of pace surprise everyone, and explain why the competition can seem "dynamic, even fierce".

Several factors have encouraged the development of hypercompetition:

– the increasing requirements of consumers, who want ever-better quality at ever-lower prices;

– information technologies, which make it possible to penetrate markets more easily through greater access and control of information;

– companies from countries with low wage costs or assistance from governments who are willing to lose money for a certain time in order to occupy new niches;

– the removal of institutional barriers to access in most countries.

It should also be noted[1] that the American stock market prefers companies from sectors where rivalry among competitors is fiercest. This contrasts with what happened in the past, when the value of a firm decreased with increasing competition. Now, however, the opposite is true, no doubt because with the price war, the quest for innovation and aggressive advertising, firms subjected to hypercompetition have reached an unequalled level of competitiveness.

---

1. Please see the study by L. G. Thomas in *Organization Science* on 200 sectors and over 3,000 companies, June 1996.

As the company is no longer separate from its environment, it is becoming an active organization that has no frontiers. Globalization, by making it possible to gain access to new markets thanks to progress in transportation and communication technology, regulations and governments' policies and has abolished geographical boundaries and has thus broadened competition. Simultaneously, the new information and communication technologies, which have been developing spectacularly, have not only been a means to increase flexibility and productivity, but have also forced people to rethink the way they organize their firms. It is clear that in order to survive, the qualities to be developed are flexibility and creativity.

In addition, it has become apparent that the quest for excellence[1] is becoming a priority. However, it must be known that this excellence is transitory and should be called into question at all times.

Hi-Tech Economy[2]

Available statistics confirm that ICT (information and communication technology) and their applications in production are having an increasingly significant effect on the economy as a whole. As a sector, they carry great macroeconomic weight (some 8% of the GNP) and they are growing on average at double the rate of other sectors. Much of the health of the US economy can be explained, for some analysts, by the growth of "hi-tech" economy. However, this diagnosis is still questionable, and is difficult to evaluate accurately.

The impact on productivity in ICT companies does not appear clearly in official statistics[3]. The most commonly suggested explanation is that the statistics bear mostly on the service sector, for which the assessment mechanisms are inappropriate, since they are based on methods designed for industry rather than the service-dominated modern world. In addition, qualitative changes introduced following innovations are generally not taken into consideration fully enough as they do not result in new products, only different practices. Finally, ICT requires a certain initiation period to

---

1. R. T. Pascale, *Managing on the Edge*, 1990.

2. On this point, see M. Guillaume and D. Roux, L'économie hi-tech (The High-Tech Economy), in *Espérances et menaces de l'an 2000*, (Hopes and Threats in 2000) Paris, Descartes & Cie, 1999.

3. R. Solow (Nobel Prize 1987) stated as long ago as 1987 in the *New York Times* that computers were everywhere except in official statistics.

become efficient, and this takes time. Having access to a computer is not enough to improve productivity. Software and complementary technologies are also necessary, and the staff has to know how to use them; mastering any new technology can take years. Nevertheless, it appears that under the influence of these new tools, most activities are shifting towards a context in which intellectual work is taking over from manual work, and constant innovation is replacing repetitive mass production.

Any productive process requires, among other factors, technical, commercial and accounting information. For many years, the processing of such information was relegated to second place. Things changed some forty years ago with the shift from Taylorism to Toyotism[1], when it was discovered that information, when managed more efficiently, made it possible to produce in a shorter time, with less stock, fewer defects and therefore improved quality. This improved management is based on two principles:

– individual productivity is important, but overall productivity is the final objective;

– the various departments of a company, which spontaneously tend to develop according to their own logic, must constantly be refocused on the customer.

These two ideas dismiss the received wisdom: individual excellence or the excellence of a department is not enough to ensure optimum performance for the company as a whole. The simple or hierarchical decentralization of information that characterizes the Taylorist model wastes all the intelligence that a system may acquire on itself and on its environment.

This acquisition requires an improvement in the information system and the transformation of forms of organization and management methods into network structures, operating across the board and less confined by hierarchy[2].

---

1. Toyotism is a form of working organization devised in the 1950s by Taiichi Ohno, an engineer at the Japanese firm Toyota, and imitated by western firms in the 1980s. It is based on a number of essential principles: "just-in-time" production (no stock), the independence of individual agents, the interactivity of posts, the flexibility and transverse structure of working organization and the versatility of the staff.

2. The *kanban* system, on which Toyotism is based, and which largely initiated total quality policies, is grounded in a system of information that, despite its archaic appearance, prefigures today's information systems in many industrial sectors.

The development of means of communication and commutation heralds a new phase, and the company itself is becoming commutative. These two shifts, the emergence of new communication tools and gradual changes in the organization of companies, work in harmony. The first facilitates and accelerates the second, though it is not its only cause.

Companies which use the Internet and its derivatives (Intranet and Extranet) are discovering ways of gathering together internal and external communications around a single protocol using networks with no boundaries. They are also discovering that these mechanisms enable them to analyze their clientele more efficiently.

New Organization, New Management

In order to rise to the new challenges facing companies, innovation is becoming the general rule in all systems of management and concerns products and services as well as production techniques and relations with the environment, not to mention organization itself.

A managerial revolution has been developing in recent years, tending to alter the very nature of work organization. Consequently, new concepts have arisen and are being implemented all over the world.

For several years already, customer-focused management methods had been used, such as "total quality" and "just-in-time" practices.

Total quality management (TQM) has as its prime goal the long-term success of the company, privileging the involvement of all the components of the organization in improving production processes, products and behavior patterns;

The "just-in-time" system, still referred to as "tight flow", owes its conception to Toyota's Taiichi Ohno, and consists in eliminating as far as possible all wastage in terms of materials, time and labor, thus obtaining the famous configuration of zero stock, zero defect and zero turnaround time. Arising from this there is obviously a new concept of the company, with the implementation of new management systems, reduction in stocks and the reorganization of the management of the various flows.

However, after these first managerial innovations, things developed even further. During the 1980s, countless models were designed. Some of them provided real solutions to the problems companies were encountering, but others were just common-sense formulae answering none of the new questions most decision makers were raising.

All these new concepts have led to a major revolution in the management of companies with the following effects:

– reduction in staffing levels ("downsizing") has been recommended so as to make companies more "lean";

– the abandonment of hierarchical strata ("delayering" or "flattening") has been implemented so as to transform companies into "horizontal" corporations;

– delegating power to various staff members ("empowerment") aims at developing a "learning" organization;

– non-core businesses must be sold in order to concentrate on the core business, and this relies on outsourcing and network organization.

It must be acknowledged that these practices, although often merely based on common sense, have given new vitality to a great many companies, both in Europe and the United States.

Reinventing Businesses

From this new environment a new type of company has arisen, streamlined and flexible, aiming to limit internal operations to strategic skills and outsource the rest by entrusting it to suppliers, subcontractors and external partners.

The company can be represented as a central nucleus giving impetus to a network made up of the best suppliers in the world. Thus the company concentrates on what it does best, and grows rapidly and regularly launches new products with less capital and slimmed-down management structures.

The two words which best characterize how today's companies function are *flexibility* and *responsiveness*. This new-style company is first and foremost focused on the customer, produces swiftly and well, and makes extensive use of information and communication technologies. However, to attain these objectives, it was necessary to reconsider production processes and management methods, starting from scratch through reengineering, setting up a new organization with fewer, yet more versatile, hierarchical strata, focusing on its core business and outsourcing more and more operations, thereby increasing flexibility.

No company, however big it is, can continue to operate only internally. It will have to concentrate on its key skills, and its core

business will have to call more and more frequently upon more efficient partners for other tasks. A new mode of organization has
arisen, and this will call into question a number of the postulates on
the basis of which management has developed.

Finally, it must be underlined that globalization makes it possible
to extend competition to producers the world over. This encourages
all of them to do better than the others, to offer goods and services
that are both cheaper and of better quality. As Friedrich von Hayek
(Nobel Prize 1974) observed, competition is a process of discovery
that is a major factor in innovation.

In this new environment, everyone stands to win. Poor or less
developed countries can obtain at low cost goods and services
essential to their development, and the richer countries can
improve their performance by giving business to firms based in
countries where costs are lower. By opening up to the world, Tai-
wan has developed; by withdrawing into its shell, North Korea has
moved down the path to stagnation and even recession.

CHAPTER 2 :

THE RETURN TO CORE BUSINESS

One of the main objectives of economics is to study the ways in which rare resources are used. As John Hicks (Nobel Prize in Economics, 1972) has shown[1], two mechanisms make this allocation possible: procurement (or redistribution) and exchange (or the market). In other words, an economic transaction takes place within a company or group following a hierarchical decision[2], or *via* a market by means of a contract.

In the first case, decisions in a purely administrative or authoritarian manner, whereas in the second, i.e. in the case of the market, the economic agents concerned make free choices based on a system of pricing.

For a long time now, these two systems have coexisted in our economies, procurement and its corollary distribution being intended to correct the malfunctions of a market that nonetheless makes the system effective.

In terms of microeconomics, these two modes of resource allocation can be found, though on different terms. However, carrying out a transaction invariably implies costs. On the markets, these costs are incurred by the search for information on prices and the signing of contracts between buyers and sellers. Within the company, defining the procedures applicable to these exchanges also incurs costs. It

---

1. John Hicks (1904-1989), British economist. See *A Theory of Economic History*, 1969, Oxford, Clarendon Press.
2. O.E. Williamson, *Markets and Hierarchies*, Free Press, New York, 1975.

must also be added that companies are entities that engage in commercial exchange with their environments, but within them transactions are made administratively. This particular situation has given rise to much discussion of the question of the very existence of companies and consideration of the role of their internal organization.

Market or Company?

Why do companies exist?[1] This apparently banal question is nonetheless essential. It was asked by Ronald Coase (Nobel Prize 1991) as long ago as 1937 in a now famous article entitled *The Nature of the Firm*. In this article, the Nobel Prize laureate-to-be wondered why such stable and organized structures as companies were appearing in a world in which the allocation of rare resources was overwhelmingly determined by the market. In his view, within companies, a complex structure of market exchange is replaced by the coordinating entrepreneur managing production.

The existence of companies is essentially explained by the difficulty in allocating a given resource *via* the market, specifically the labor factor, and market transactions presuppose the signing of either short- or long-term contracts.

Acquiring the labor factor necessary to production on the basis of short-term contracts (valid for a day, for example) is inefficient due to the high cost of repeating the operation daily[2], and the use of long-term contracts is almost impossible. In order to ensure that the execution of a contract is not open to dispute, the rights and obligations of the parties must be defined with great accuracy. This is impossible when there is a question of accurately setting out, for a period of one year, for example, what sales staff must do in all imaginable circumstances.

This is why allocation of labor is based on individual contracts. The seller agrees, in return for remuneration determined in advance, to follow the instructions issued by the buyer within a given context. Thus there is a voluntarily accepted hierarchical relationship that is one of the characteristics of a company.

---

1. Ronald Coase, born in 1910, British economist, Nobel Prize in Economics, 1991, *The Nature of the Firm*, Economica, vol. 4, 1937.

2. This general rule still has some exceptions in practice. Longshoremen are traditionally hired on a short-term basis (often day-to-day). This practice is in no way a guarantee of the economic efficiency of the procedure.

An Example of Transaction Costs

Take the example of a car salesman. He could theoretically operate alone, buying cars from manufacturers, taking on the services of an agent to store the vehicles before selling them and calling upon a specialized company to transport them from factory to warehouse and deliver them to the customer, etc. As these operations require a certain number of administrative tasks, another specialized company has to be brought in to file mail, write letters, take calls and so on. In addition, an accountant has to be hired to keep the books.

The classic theory ensures that all these transactions are carried out at the most advantageous cost by playing rival suppliers off against one another, thus making use of the market mechanisms.

However, it may also be considered that to reduce costs, it may be advisable for the car salesman to rent premises to store the vehicles, to recruit a warehouseman, a secretary and an accountant, and to deliver the cars to customers himself. In other words, by setting up a company carrying out all these operations, it is conceivable to arrive at costs lower than the total sum resulting from the various exchanges on the market: the salesman has become a car dealer.

The company founder thus plays the role of "coordinator" and replaces the market mechanisms, since it is no longer necessary to determine prices for each of the transactions carried out. For example, a number of long-term contracts can be drawn up for the secretary, the warehouseman and the storage premises, replacing the chain of short-term contracts drawn up on the market.

If the exchange of goods and services on the market were the most efficient and most economical means to allocate resources, there would be no point in the company recruiting staff, setting up a production line or an accounts department, since all the functions of the company could be contracted out and carried out by other firms.

Thus, contrary to more recent market theories, if a company turns to the market to meet its supply needs, whatever they may be, it will incur transactional costs, such as costs arising from information, negotiation, the drafting of contracts and supervision of their execution. These costs can be grouped into two main categories:

– The cost of relevant information, as since market information is inadequate because of the uncertain environment, acquiring it is costly. For Ronald Coase, the main reason that makes setting up a company advantageous is apparently the existence of a cost for the use of the pricing mechanism. The most obvious expenditure for the organization of production through the pricing mechanism arises from the search for appropriate prices. This expenditure may be reduced, though not eliminated, by the activities of specialized agents gathering and selling this information.

– Other costs, which are essentially related to the negotiation and conclusion of contracts, of which there are more and more as exchange increases.

For example, in a market-based system, each agent taking part in production must negotiate and conclude separate contracts for each transaction. If 10 people take part in a given project, 45 (10 × 9 divided by 2)[1] contracts binding the various agents need to be signed, and naturally all these operations involve expenditure.

As mentioned above, the main reason that makes setting up a company advantageous is apparently the existence of a cost for the use of the pricing mechanism. This implies that the company is becoming an alternative method of allocating resources, which gains a footing as it is more efficient. Within a company, it is not necessary to fix a price for each internal exchange; turnaround is more reliable and internal coordination means saving money compared to going onto the market.

By internalizing, i.e. by not going through the market, a company can organize its contracts around a given number of agents exercising authority, which reduces the number of contracts necessary to ensure production. The 10 entities that previously had to sign 45 contracts to coordinate with market requirements now only need to sign 9 agreements with persons acting on behalf of the company for a limited period of time.

This logic explains vertical incorporation, when coordination is more advantageous than resorting to the market. By demonstrating that it is more efficient – which is to say, less costly – to allocate resources administratively (within the company) rather than through a pricing system (*via* the market), Ronald Coase explains the emergence of companies. To paraphrase Coase, firms are rafts of sensible coordination floating on a sea of commercial relations like curds in whey. As this process becomes more widespread, it is also easier to understand why most of them diversify, since what is true for a single product is still true when the firm produces several.

---

1. 10 × 9 divided by 2, as contracts need to be signed by all participants. A with B, then on to C; B with A, C and D, and so forth.

It is thus preferable to have a single firm making several products than a group of firms each producing only one.

The Limits of the Firm

Problems of coordination and the costs inherent to the existence of a hierarchy mean that beyond a certain volume of transactions, the cost of their administrative organization rises swiftly. However, it may initially be assumed that on the market, the costs remain stable.

The number of transactions carried out is linked not only to the size of the company by also to the diversity of its operations. As long as the marginal cost of the administrative organization is lower than the market cost, the transaction should take place within the company. However, beyond a certain size, there is greater advantage in proceeding with exchanges on the market, i.e. between individual companies.

There remains the question of why companies and the market continue to coexist, while the first method of organizing the economic process is more efficient than the second. The answer to this depends more on intuition (though based on deduction) than on rigorous analysis. Coase considers that as a company increases in size, the marginal cost of internal transactions also grows, and that sooner or later it will be equal to that of exchanges taking place on the market. In this case, it is more advantageous to use the second option.

Two main arguments have been used to support this theory. The first is that beyond a certain size, management yields fall, due both to the difficulty in organizing additional transaction and to increasingly inefficient allocation of production factors. The second is that the cost of certain factors (principally labor) can increase with size, as the non-monetary advantages (nature of responsibilities, freedom of action, control procedures, etc.) linked with employment are greater in small companies than in larger firms. This discourse, to a certain premonitory degree, is not, unfortunately, supported by convincing reasoning.

However, such pioneering work should not be criticized for having certain gaps and weaknesses. Coase is still a major author, and he paved the way for research that has made it possible to understand better not only what a company really is, but also certain aspects of its operating methods.

Beyond Mere Transaction Costs

Oliver Williamson[1] took Coase's analysis one step further, studying more accurately the very nature of transaction costs. These are linked to the complexity and uncertainty of the environment and to various human factors, notably the limited rationality of the agents concerned and their individualistic and opportunistic behavior.

For Williamson, the dysfunction within markets can be explained by the convergence of factors dependent on the environment and of the behavior patterns of the decision makers themselves. More precisely, the combination of the uncertainty and complexity of the environment with the limited rationality of the agents concerned, and that of the small number of decision-makers given to opportunism, hinder the smooth running of exchanges on the markets.

The concept of limited rationality that Williamson uses came to light through the work of Herbert Simon[2] (Nobel Prize in Economics 1978), who considers that economic agents do not act according to the principle of maximization. A given individual can only absorb, store and process a limited amount of information, since their neurophysiological capacities are themselves finite. Furthermore, human language is also limited, and there is not always a means of expression making it possible to pass on knowledge, instructions or sentiments to others with no ambiguity. Thus, contracts regulating relations between individuals can only be imperfect, since no one can definitely predict the decisions made by the other parties.

However, it must be pointed out that these limits to rationality only play a restrictive role in situations where the environment is highly uncertain and complex. In this case, it is difficult, or even impossible to draft contracts providing for all possible situations and how to react to them. This is why the administrative organization of a company leads to making noticeable savings in comparison with limited rationality. Consequently, in theory it is no longer

---

1. Oliver Williamson, born in 1932, American economist, Professor at the University of California, Berkeley, developed his analysis in three major publications: *Markets and Hierarchies*, Free Press, 1975; *The Economic Institutions of Capitalism*, Free Press, New York, 1985; *Strategizing, Economizing and Economic Organization*, in *Strategic Management Journal*, Winter 1993.

2. Herbert Simon (1916-2001), American economist, Nobel Prize in Economics 1978.

necessary to predict all possible events; it is enough to concentrate on those which actually occur, or which are highly likely to occur.

– Opportunism (meaning the effort to make individual profits beyond the normal income arising from exchange) alters the classic hypothesis according to which economic agents strive for maximum utility by introducing strategic considerations, for example resorting to cunning. One manifestation of opportunistic behavior consists in making promises without having the slightest intention of keeping them, or making threats that will never be carried out.

– When there are a large number of players, this type of behavior has no impact on the market, since the opportunists will be eliminated on the renewal of short-term contracts. However, when there are few players involved (monopoly or oligopoly), this is no longer the case. In this instance the firms present on the market do well to act to encourage the maximization of joint profits. When profits are shared out – a no-win, no-gain situation for buyers and sellers – each party is tempted to obtain the greatest advantage by whatever means possible, this leading to long and costly negotiation processes prejudicial to all firms. The market thus becomes an inefficient method of resource allocation.

– Williamson has extended his analysis, taking into account phenomena linked with technological indivisibility, emphasizing the relationship between the specific nature of investments and the dysfunctioning of the market.

– An asset is deemed to be specific when it only makes it possible to produce particular goods or services intended for a single customer. This specific characteristic thus lies in the transaction rather than merely in the production. When the asset is not highly specific, the costs of seeking out (on the market) an appropriate external partner and of setting up the transaction can be very low, while the cost of a possible internal transaction will always be at least equal to the required structural minimum.

– However, if the asset is highly specific, the cost of the internal transaction is barely greater than previously, whereas the external costs (resorting to the market) soon increase considerably.

It may be said that the existence of specific assets is binding to both the seller and the buyer, the first because the range on offer is limited to a single product, and the second because only one supplier is able to meet such specific needs. In reality, several variants on these examples can be found.

Williamson raises explicitly the question of the choice between internalization and externalization, meaning resorting to the market. Thus, for example, when manufacturing computer equipment, the question raised is whether the manufacture of the required individual components should be carried out internally or not. Williamson considers that this depends on the specific nature of the component: for standard components the answer is no, for specific components the answer is yes.

It must be added that specific investments take many forms. They may consist in equipment, but also in production unit or outlet localization, staff training or intelligence gathering.

Not only does taking transaction costs and specific assets into account make it possible to explain the emergence of organizational methods for economic activity other than the market, but it also paves the way for the analysis of different forms of internal structure adopted by companies: functional, multidivisional, adaptable, innovative, etc.

The Advantages of Integration

Following on from the ideas and concepts outlined above, a widespread move towards vertical integration started to develop after the Second World War, consisting in internalizing sales transactions as much as possible. Exchanges (sales or purchases) that used to take place on the market were now being carried out within companies.

The expected advantages to be gained from such a policy may be divided into three broad categories: the reduction of costs and the attainment of greater economic efficiency; the development of aspects of strategic domination over non-integrated competitors; and the elimination of certain dysfunctions on the market.

– The reduction of costs and the improved performance of companies can be explained by two major factors. The first is the existence of more efficient coordination of activities at the various stages of the transformation process than in the case of two independent firms. The famous example of this is hot rolling in the iron and steel industry. If a single company runs simultaneously a steel plant and a rolling train on the same site, it can make considerable savings on energy costs. With such a system, it does not have to wait until the ingots have cooled to transport them to the mill train, then having to reheat them to turn them into sheet metal. The ingots can be thus rolled as soon as they leave the plant, before they have time to cool down. This example also partly explains why vertical integration is so common in activities using continuous flow techniques, such as the chemical and petrochemical industries.

The superiority of integrated companies over independent firms is that for them it is possible to achieve greater harmony between individual activities and the various stages of the production process. It must be added that advantages can be gained in terms of both production or stock management costs and investment policies (balanced growth in capacities at different levels) or research and development (improvement in the flow of information between laboratories, or concentration of activities). A further advantage in terms of cost has often been inaccurately described as controlling or securing supplies or outlets. The effects of vertical integration are economic rather than physical. If an oil company has, for example, its own pipelines in the Persian Gulf or in Iraq, it is no better protected from risks of breakdowns or sabotage than an independent company. However, in certain circumstances, the integration policy can have beneficial effects on the levels of purchasing or product sales prices. This is the case when the markets on which the company purchases its supplies or sells its products are fundamentally imperfect, since the prices are not determined by the classic mechanisms of supply and demand. Vertical integration affords protection from the power of buyers or sellers[1].

– There are occasionally strategic issues linked with vertical integration. These appear when integrated firms are in competition with non-integrated companies. The latter thus find themselves competing with organizations which are also either customers or suppliers. The former can make the most of their favorable position to lower their prices ("squeeze" policy) and gain competitive – though illegitimate – advantage over non-integrated firms. An example of this is Alcoa, which, between the wars, was the only aluminum producer in the United States. It rolled part of its production and sold the rest to independent processors at prices significantly higher than normal, given the costs involved. It was never possible to prove this practice before the courts, and Alcoa was dismantled because of its monopolistic position.

---

1. A counter-example is that there are no integrated firms involved in both the production and processing of copper. The reason is that since the middle of the 19th century there has been a market for this metal that operates in conditions resembling pure, perfect competition. Producers and users of copper would make no savings in terms of price through respectively downstream and upstream integration.

– One final advantage of vertical integration is to compensate for certain dysfunctions on the markets, by making it possible to carry out transactions that may take place within market mechanisms. The problem is connected with the existence of specific production assets, both material and immaterial, which is to say so specialized that under satisfactory economic conditions, all they can do is produce single goods or services intended for a single customer, or a very small number of customers. In such a situation, market mechanisms work far from perfectly. Should the buyer wish to obtain the intermediary product or service he requires, or should the seller wish to clear his stocks, the only option available is to adopt vertical integration. An example of this is provided by research and development activities. There are very few companies producing only the results of research, these results then being sold on to other firms for commercial use[1]. In such cases, these organizations market patents or production techniques, but these are evidently rare. This can be explained by the specific characteristics of research activities, the products of which are rarely used by those having financed the projects themselves. For this reason, most applied research, resulting in immediately useable discoveries, is carried out within the companies that have initiated it, and whose purpose it is to make such investment profitable.

The Limits of Vertical Integration

Vertical integration does not only have advantages. If this were the case, all companies would be integrated. This policy comes up against four major categories of limit: (i) the increase in the size of the company; (ii) the growth in rigid structures; (iii) the risk of atrophy; and (iv) the incompatibility between products (negative synergy).

– Like diversification, vertical integration leads to an increase in the sizes of companies, which, while bringing certain advantages, also tends to make internal management procedures more cumbersome and less efficient. In such cases, there is a heightened risk of increasing bureaucracy.

---

1. One partial exception is universities. However, these are not trading organizations, and frequently research projects are initiated and financed by third parties (public bodies or private companies).

– Secondly, vertical integration often leads to increasing inflexibility in the management of the company by augmenting the ratio of fixed costs. Purchases made outside the company may be modulated according to the fluctuations in the firm's production. Thus these largely make up the variable costs. This is no longer true when the company produces certain of the intermediate items it then processes. Generally speaking, the investments made to produce these items make it possible to reduce average costs on condition that the volume of production is sufficient to make use of potential economies of scale. Vertical integration exaggerates, both upwards and downwards, the impact of fluctuations in the company's activities on its results. A reduction in the ultimate demand may thus have extremely nefarious consequences on profitability, and even call the firm's survival into question. This explains the disappearance of the *Saturday Evening Post*. Founded at the beginning of the 20th century, the *Post* had become, with a circulation of several million, the biggest-selling American newspaper. Instead of jumping at new opportunities that were offered to it, such as the buyout of CBS, the *Post* implemented a total integration policy, from forest exploitation and paper manufacture to printing and distribution. When the *Post*'s sales faltered, the whole of the chain was affected, and in a few years the empire had collapsed.

– Another limit to the integration policy is the risk of atrophy. If all exchanges take place within the firm, the intermediary stages are isolated from their immediate external environment and protected from the competition, which leads to the loss of often stimulating pressure. Efficiency incentives, both in terms of short-term costs and in terms of the long-term adaptation of products to developments in the environment, are thus significantly less pressing than for a company permanently up against not only its competitors but also suppliers and independent customers, and under threat from the emergence of substitute products. This type of situation tends to lead to a certain laxness, and may even result in serious strategic errors. This was the case, for example, for General Motors, which spent tens of millions of dollars improving the performance of drum brakes and building a production line to manufacture them. At the same time – in the late 1950s – European manufacturers were starting systematically to fit their cars with disc brakes.

The negative effects of these last two disadvantages – rigid structures and the risk of atrophy – may be reduced if the integrated company adopts certain practices in internal organization. The principle is to reintroduce competition mechanisms into the company, be they in simulated or actual form.

One option is to grant the status of profit center to each level of the processing chain and, for example, to bring internal transfer prices into line with the market prices of identical products or authorize external sales or purchases. If the results were to be negative, this would be evidence of poor management, as independent firms have shown themselves capable of surviving in similar pricing conditions. In such a context, the long-term advantages of integration and the short-term benefits of competition come together.

Another hurdle can be overcome if the different stages are effectively allowed to procure supplies or to sell on the market. In such a case, within the integrated company, it is possible to set up true-to-life competitive conditions, sometimes known as open integration. The autonomy granted in both cases to the stages of the production process implies, in order to achieve the desired effects, the decentralization of the decision-making powers. In principle, this is not highly compatible with the existence of a single coordination centre, the latter being one of the major advantages of vertical integration.

Finally, it should be noted that one of the major problems raised by vertical integration is the compatibility of products. There is a significant risk that negative synergies may appear among the various activities, which would then reduce the overall efficiency of the integrated firm. One such situation arose in an integrated company in the aluminum sector, specializing in the processing of the metal and associated finished products. One of its end-stage activities was to produce aluminum foil, for which the market was highly competitive. At this level, one of the requirements for survival was to reduce costs, which implied reducing the quantity of metal incorporated into the foil. However, one stage upstream, where the sheet metal was produced, the major performance criterion was the volume of sales. The objectives of the two stages being incompatible with each other, the company was forced to give up aluminum foil production.

Questioning a System

Most frequently, the negative consequences of these integration methods were only of secondary importance during the post-war period of rapid growth of western economies. However, they are now taking center stage in today's circumstances, notably due to globalization and hypercompetition. Certain vertical integration policies are thus now being questioned. Firms are growing apart from those of their production lines that are showing negative synergy with the activities they wish to continue with, thus opting for a reorientation policy. However, the questioning of such a system may also be involuntary and unexpected, in the form of a hostile take-over bid aiming at dismantling the company concerned. Restructuring operations and hostile take-over bids have been particularly frequent in recent years.

Given its limits, vertical integration is no panacea for the dysfunctions of the market. This is why companies increasingly resort to new organizational methods.

For Williamson, the integration of a large number of functions within a single structure makes it possible to save on the transaction costs generated by the market (those linked to uncertainty, negotiation or lack of information on prices). As a counter-example, the force of the market resides in its motivation mechanisms, which companies are unable to reproduce. Nor should it be forgotten that integration entails administration costs, implying that it cannot be taken too far. It is thus necessary to weigh up these different costs so as to determine the right level of specialization and integration.

For example, a few years ago Tenneco, Inc., one of the largest conglomerates in the United States with a payroll of over 100,000, acquired Houston Oil, a small oil company with 1,200 employees. Tenneco offered particular financial advantages to the most experienced staff in Houston Oil in order to keep them. In spite of this, a large number of Houston Oil's executives left the company for various reasons: bureaucratic delays in setting up the new pay deals, problems with setting up differential treatment in the name of internal equity, not forgetting the offers from independent producers able to offer the workers substantial financial advantages. In Williamson's view, large companies are not always able, despite their efforts, to do the same as small companies.

At all events, the balance between integration and outsourcing is one of today's most pressing questions in the management of modern companies: what should be produced in-house and what should be outsourced? It should be added that the conditions relating to competition and the environment have led to the equation being considered in other ways than in the past. The decision between market and outsourcing rests on the choice between the incentive-inducing force of the market mechanisms and the adaptability arising from the discretionary powers of the hierarchy within the company. In more recent works, Williamson has underscored the existence of hybrid forms of organization, borrowing aspects both from market mechanisms and hierarchical structures. Such companies could be described as partnership-based or contractual: alliances, joint ventures, franchises and transactional firms, for example. They are less costly than hierarchical organizations due to the savings they make possible. They also incur lower costs than the market thanks to savings on transactional costs.

The Impact of Information and Communication Technologies

Information technologies are present in all sections of a company, be they in logistics subsystems or management subsystems, and their role keeps on growing. This whole phenomenon is based on the improvement of technical performance (processing and memory capacity, speed of execution, etc.) in the processing and transfer of information, alongside a dramatic reduction in costs.

However, these considerations are not enough to explain the arrival *en masse* of these technologies in companies. A key factor in their success is the increasing user-friendliness of the systems installed (hardware and software packages), so that non-specialists are not only able to use them but actually agree to do so.

The many advantages linked to these technologies are significant. Things run more efficiently, meaning more rapidly and at a lower cost, than before, the classic example being the automation of repetitive tasks. And the range of possibilities is broadening; it is now possible to do things we did not know how to do, or were simply physically impossible before. This can be illustrated by the setting-up of real-time quality control procedures in the production process. In the management field, in-depth transformations are taking place both within the company and in its relationship with its environment.

The increasing efficiency of management processes along with the emergence of new products and new activities is making a highly positive contribution thanks to the development of computers and telecommunications.

The development of techniques connected with information and communication has led not only to changes in the way various activities in the value chain are carried out, but also to the emergence of new opportunities for research or action. Furthermore, this has often resulted in strong links being forged between stages that were previously independent. Computerization makes possible considerable growth in the volume of information taken into account, notably thanks to an increase in memory capacity and in speed of processing. For example, it has been estimated that between 1958 and 1980 the time required to carry out an elementary electronic operation was divided by 80 million[1], and since then equally if not more significant progress has been made. Reliability has also noticeably increased; data recording methods – for example bar codes – have reduced the margin for error by a ratio of 10,000 to 1. Finally, it is now possible to use qualitative information to build up databases or to develop tailor-made systems.

It should also be added that the combination of computing and telecommunications has the twofold advantage of reducing spatial constraints and – to a lesser extent and in the short term – those of temporal coordination thanks to permanent safeguarding. It makes it possible to replace the movements of staff, material resources or products by transfers of information or to improve speed and reliability. The advantages that can be gained are considerable, and take a variety of forms: reductions in costs, shorter turnaround, close coordination among activities and more efficient use of the resources available.

A New Generation of Companies

The last few years have seen the emergence of a new generation of companies, less bureaucratic, more flexible and essentially oriented towards their core businesses. The objective is no longer – as was the case in the 1960s – to integrate as many functions as possible, but to limit internal operations to the key skill or skills that they have, and to let the market do the rest, meaning suppliers, partners or subcontractors.

In the late 19th century, electricity was considered a means of encouraging the return to working from home or in small workshops. Over the last few years, with the emergence of information and communication technologies (ICT), the discourse is similar. These technologies are seen as a decisive factor, making it possible for companies to reorient their operations, to circulate information and to open up to the outside world.

---

1. M. Porter and V. Millar, How information gives you competitive advantage, *Harvard Business Review*, spring 1985.

For some ten years now, many companies all over the world have been rethinking their production processes, since a vertically integrated company that organizes its entire value chain internally is subject to two highly prejudicial limitations:

– First, as seen above, this type of firm cannot attain an optimum level for each of its functions. There is no point in having the most modern factories and the most brilliant sales team if the logistics or even the switchboard are mediocre.

How Companies Have Developed

1. **"Transactional organization"**: in this case, allocation of resources is effected within the markets. This type of micro-firm was the most widespread model in the Middle Ages.

2. **"Integrated organization"**: here, allocation of resources is effected internally, this being the classic company. Coase's model firm, in which as many function as possible are internalized, developed from the 18th century to the 1990s.

3. **"Outsourcing-based organization"**: allocation of resources is improved thanks to subcontracting, and the firm is open to the outside world.

4. **"Network-based or virtual organization"**: the return to core business, recourse to strategic outsourcing, leading to "Laborgistics®".

– Second, if all stages of value creation are carried out internally, structural adaptation capacities are limited, since all operatives, from the top to the bottom of the ladder, wish to justify, defend or ensure the survival of their activities.

Integrated companies are efficient when the product is standardized, manufactured in great quantities and stabilized for a number of years. However, the context today has changed, and the keyword dominating the market is "flexibility". The companies that will survive are those that will be able to adapt rapidly to technological change, to fickle consumers and to new competitors. More room should be given to markets than to hierarchies.

These new companies are described in various ways, although they have certain characteristics in common or at least similar objectives. There follows an outline of network companies or transactional companies, and modular companies or virtual companies. The end result is a set of models that while ill-defined are naturally described as the companies of the future.

The Network Company

This type of company is seen as a set of units communicating with each other, with the common goal of satisfying an increasingly demanding clientele. The very concept of these firms rests on such notions as autonomy and responsibility, thus enabling them to react to events rather than pre-established rules. These companies are in close contact with the market, which enables them to be run in an "entrepreneurial" spirit, and also to adapt rapidly to any changes in their environment. This is a situation in which several companies maintain long-term relationships, and thus are at an intermediate level between individual firm and market.

Network companies, which some prefer to refer to as "transactional companies", are defined as structures with independent capital within a single chain of added value. An emblematic example is the famous company Benetton, founded in 1965, with 6,000 internal staff but that employs a further 60,000 in 450 subcontracted companies. The same is true of Toyota, which produces 70 cars per worker, as opposed to 10 for General Motors. This difference does not stem from productivity, but from the outsourcing rate. Around Toyota there are almost 10,000 subcontracting companies in a pyramidal arrangement known as *kyoryoku-kai*.

The company thus becomes a center around which revolves a network of subcontracting firms, and as a result the boundaries of the company itself become blurred. Furthermore, the nature of the relationships with the environment (competitors, customers, suppliers, the state) changes, since more and more frequently these companies conclude agreements with their suppliers. It all comes down to the fact that these network companies have two major foundations: outsourcing and alliances.

– Through outsourcing, one or more functions are delegated to external service providers for a limited period of time. It should be added that almost all of these functions are likely to be outsourced, and that this use of partners external to the company is often made in countries where labor costs are low.

At the same time, this reorientation towards core business gives rise to specialization, which leads to greater effectiveness procuring several advantages:
- it favors reductions in costs;
- it speeds up the development of new products;
- it reduces underused capacities;

– it concentrates resources on activities making it possible to obtain a competitive edge.

All this leads to a value chain made up of a set of either independent companies or companies interdependent in relation to suppliers, who play a major part and whose loyalty it is important to ensure.

It must also be noted that outsourcing is a steadily-growing phenomenon for two reasons:

– As consumers are looking for increasingly personalized products, companies must take into account greater segmentation of markets and thus produce limited series, which are more costly.

– Since the return on investment in the industrial sector is lower than in the service sector, manufacturers are being forced to reduce their capital intensity through outsourcing.

More and more alliances are being formed, in order to pool resources (notably new technologies), aiming to break into new markets. These improve reaction time, one of the biggest assets in modern companies, enabling them to develop new products, perfect new processes or acquire licenses more quickly.

These convergences can take on many forms, from mergers and acquisitions to joint ventures and partnerships. However, it should be noted that despite the advantages they bring, alliances also present risks that may eventually lead to a loss of skills within a company's core business.

The efficiency of a network depends on the relations between the different components of the organization, and may become apparent on three levels: loyalty, the nature of management techniques and steering methods.

– All networks are dependent on the personnel making them up and running them, thus there should be a certain complicity among them. Over time, a network progresses and fills out, but it can only survive if relations among the partners are founded on loyalty, eventually turning subcontractors into "co-contractors".

– On a more general level, the efficiency of operating in networks presupposes stable, well-understood procedures (such as ISO norms). It is also vital for management teams to work together, not neglecting to take into account cultural differences (for example languages, cooperative cultures and confidentiality practices). A network must be headed by a true coordinator, keeping it active by circulating information and know-how to ensure things run smoothly and make it possible to pool knowledge.

– A network can only function if these leaders are able to provide the homogenous business units with common objectives, and if steering mechanisms are set up to encourage the transverse flow of information enabling all the teams to work together.

In short, the company that was originally an organization with many decision-making centers has now become a much broader organization, taking on the form of a "fragmented" company through its burgeoning alliances and partnerships.

The Virtual Company

Thanks to the progress and development of the new technologies of communication and information, an even more original form has appeared, known as the "virtual company"[1]. It should be noted that this is a misleading title, since it conjures up the idea of virtual reality, an artificial reproduction, a sort of computerized simulation. However, these companies could not be more real, with their factories, their distribution networks, premises and personnel, although these operations are linked with separate companies.

The word "virtual" is a reference to virtual memory[2], the process through which a computer can simulate an extension of its memory by using part of its hard disk. The principle of the virtual company is the same, in that it takes advantage of resources and skills it does not possess. The difference between virtual companies and classic firms lies essentially in the definition of how they are governed and in the legal and financial tracing of their boundaries.

We can define the virtual company as "a network of independent firms pooling resources and skills thanks to information and communication technologies". This organization makes it possible to make use of resources the firm does not have in a quest for excellence. Thanks to information technology, they can find partners in databases and enter into relations with other firms even if they are

---

1. This concept was popularized by W. Dawidow and M. Malone, "The Virtual Corporation", *Business Week*, 1993.

2. The adjective "virtual" is used in computing to define a system in terms of performance and operational possibilities. For example, referring to a computer with 16 million bits of internal memory and which can run programs of 8 million bits, it is said to have an actual memory of 16 million bits and a virtual memory of 8 million bits.

geographically distant. It must be added that this type of firm has no boundaries, and that it is totally opportunistic since it is based on no formal structure. In other words, these firms spring into being to make the most of a given market, then disappear when no longer needed.

Examples of Virtual Companies

– MCC, the subsidiary of Mercedes Benz that assembles the Smart car, shares its factory in Hamback, in Lorraine (France), with its eight front-line suppliers. In addition, it has entrusted all its organization, recruitment and human resources management to Andersen Consulting.

– Calvin Klein is essentially a marketing service, selecting manufacturers of clothing, perfume, eyewear and watches.

– Nike no longer manufactures shoes internally, but subcontracts all of its production to Japan or Korea, which due to labor costs in turn outsource to China, Indonesia and Vietnam. A total of 100,000 people all over the world are manufacturing Nike products, while the company has a staff of only 5,000.

The virtual company is an organizational innovation having a certain number of advantages particularly well suited to the environment in which firms are developing today.

– The first major asset of a virtual company is its flexibility. Given its modular structure, it can react very quickly in the event of difficulties or problems, since certain partners can then simply be replaced by others. Furthermore, regarding costs, the virtual company turns fixed outgoings (salaries, rents, etc.) into variable outgoings according to the activities of its partners and subcontractors. The virtual company thus improves the fixed cost/variable cost ratio (the operating leverage), lowers its break-even point (the sales levels making it possible to cover outgoings) and becomes less sensitive to the uncertainties of the market.

In a virtual company, production capacities can thus be quickly adapted to variations in demand by sharing the drop in activity among all the strategic partners, thus avoiding often prejudicial restructuring. The same is true in the event of an economic upswing when, for example, demand can suddenly increase.

In short, in the virtual company, fixed costs frequently become variable, which is a particular advantage in the turbulent times of today, in which it is not always an easy task to make predictions.

– Secondly, companies working together in a virtual network, by pooling their orders, naturally increase their negotiation positions with regard to suppliers, which is particularly valuable for small companies.

– Finally, by bringing together the skills and capacities of several strategic partners, the virtual company can obtain powerful leverage, thus no longer being forced to commit itself to excessive expenditure.

Despite these many advantages, it should not be forgotten that virtual companies also have their limits. The first is connected with information technology. Its role is clearly essential in this type of structure, but it may give rise to a number of disadvantages or constraints, particularly the tentative acceptance of it by the staff. Nevertheless, constant progress in this field has meant that the equipment, particularly that related to long-distance communication (telecommunications), can provide services that are not only increasingly efficient by also increasingly user-friendly by incorporating the following three characteristics: interactivity, compatibility (communication between different types of equipment) and of course mobility. In addition, from a legal point of view, the virtual company is not always clearly defined, and in order to operate must adopt a complex or hybrid status. Finally, it should be emphasized that the management of a virtual company is not always simple, since it requires the coordination of agents retaining their autonomy in terms of capital, unlike traditional companies.

At all events, the virtual company is an interesting and relatively appropriate solution enabling firms to rise to the challenges of globalization and hyper competition.

The Return to Traditional Structures

Generally speaking, the network of micro-companies working on a see-as-you-go basis – meaning transactional structures – is historically the primary form of industrial organization, predating by far the development of the first companies in the 17th century Europe. Among many are the silk industry in Lyon, Florence's wool industry and steel production in Toledo, all of which were flourishing industries in the Middle Ages. But hindered by excessive transactional costs – as seen above – these entities have all but disappeared over the last three hundred years in favor of incorporated companies, supposedly traditional.

However, in recent years, as seen above, the coordination costs inherent to incorporated companies have risen sharply, given the size and diversity of firms, whereas at the same time progress in information technology has made it possible to reduce significantly the cost of transactions. Transactional structures have thus reappeared, and given their results, have become alternative solutions to integrated organizations.

Examples of Transactional Structures

– The *distretti attrezzati* (industrial areas) in central Italy, such as Prato, where tens of thousands of people work in thousands of micro-companies revolving around a dozen *lanifici* (wool mills). In Italy, the famous company Benetton founded in Ponzano Veneto (near Trevise) in 1965, has become in the space of 25 years one of the three largest garment manufacturers in the world, based on transactional organization.

– "Hollow corporations" originated in the United States, and have chosen to transfer almost all their production units abroad, to countries where labor is cheaper, for example Nike, the famous sportswear manufacturer.

– The *kyoryoku-kai* (subcontractor pyramids) in Japan operate mainly in the motor industry thanks to a plethora of subcontractors revolving around a single principal.

The Company of the Future

Over the last few years, to adapt to the new environment in which companies must develop, various organizational models have been devised, all having in common two main characteristics: the reduction in the number of hierarchical levels and the decentralization of the decision-making process.

Though not yet having been directly applied, a positive point of this conception of so-called "companies of the future" is that it raises essential questions on the changes that should be made to traditional company structures. These models include the "shamrock" model and the "cluster" or "post-hierarchical" model.

The "shamrock" model[1] submitted by Charles Handy, a professor at the London Business School, questions the traditional pyramid organization. In his model, the company may be represented as a

---

1. Charles Handy, *The Age of Unreason*, Harvard Business School Press, 1990.

three-leafed clover. At the center is a small group of key highly-qualified managers. On the first leaf are all the subcontracting operations for non-essential tasks. This outsourcing can be applied abroad, where labor costs are lower, thanks to the new information and communication technologies. On the second are the temporary or part-time staff. On the third are the operational units, the only ones to be working full-time for the company. Simultaneously, the company attempts to offload as much work as possible onto the customers, by offering them self-service options in return for lower prices.

The logic of this type of organization is to reduce the management levels and to outsource as much as possible in order to achieve maximum flexibility. It may be added, as shown below, that this type of organization is no longer a simple idealistic vision but a reality within a number of companies that try to limit their middle-management strata. This is the case for Unilever and Procter & Gamble, each of which operate with a staff of only 100.

The second model is the "cluster" or "post-hierarchical" model. This has been submitted by Daniel Quinn Mills, a professor at the Harvard Business School. In his model there is a company organized in the form of clusters (some refer to this as "starburst organization"). This implies that groups of individuals (30 to 50) work together, more or less constantly, around a nucleus comprising the management team. Other groups are made up according to the needs and the nature of the company: project groups, alliance groups, function groups, etc. The individuals who are members of these groups are naturally connected by modern communications networks.

This type of organization makes it possible to reduce the number of hierarchical levels, which are inflexible and can lead to dysfunctions, by affording greater decision-making autonomy, by giving more responsibilities to the staff and by taking advantage of diversity in expertise.

The need to transform companies so as to respond better to changes in the environment is now a constant in all firms. A recent study[1] on the transformation of companies, carried out in France by a group of CEOs at the initiative of Microsoft, provides a number of particularly interesting indications.

---

1. *Réflexions stratégiques sur la transformation des entreprises* (Strategic Reflections on Corporate Transformation, the Observatory of Chairmen and CEOs), Novamétrie and Microsoft, September 2003.

Over two thirds of company heads consider it necessary to transform their own structures, and that this transformation is central to their concerns. If this transformation is seen as a process of permanent innovation, the prevailing sentiment is that of acceleration, of speed. In short, for these business leaders, the relationship to time has altered.

With the end of ideologies, the rise of globalization, the improvement in the average level of skills and the increasingly rapid fall into obsolescence of successive managerial methods, the overarching feeling arising from this study is that there is no longer any "company model". Nevertheless, company directors gravitate around a few major types of firm that they adapt according to the circumstances.

The model of the decentralized company that gives initiative and autonomy to its business units, that encourages management processes and project running finds the greatest favor. This shows that the era of the traditional hierarchical organization that separates functional and operational staff is over, and that the matrix or multidimensional models are becoming the standard.

Companies juxtapose organizational principles borrowed from various models in what could be called an "organizational cocktail", and new notions are emerging, such as the "open" or "immaterial" company. Such companies manage a given range of operations, but concentrate on their core businesses, relocating or outsourcing an increasing number of activities. Thus the boundaries of this type of organization are becoming increasingly blurred, and doubts are cast more and more frequently. This study notes the emergence of more and more virtual organizations that outsource almost all their activities, only effectively steering the operation as a whole.

The age of definitive models that can be transposed to any given situation is over. However, it must be noted that information technologies play an essential role in these changes, and that in certain cases they form the very hub of the company.

CHAPTER 3 :

TO DO IT, OR TO HAVE IT DONE – THAT IS THE QUESTION

Globalization, the opening of markets, deregulation, growing competition, an increasingly "turbulent" environment and constantly evolving technological progress... are all factors that go to make up the new context in which companies operate today. This is why these companies have to reconsider their operating methods by striving for as much organizational flexibility as possible[1]. All companies now tend to turn to the market rather than carry out the increasing number of tasks internally.

From this point of view, Nike, the famous sports footwear manufacturer, is an emblematic example. The company has retained under its direct control only strategic management, design and sales activities. The rest, i.e. the manufacture and distribution of the products, has been entirely entrusted to outside service providers. This new mode of organization is no longer exceptional. On the contrary, it is developing in many sectors and countries.

This is why all company directors regularly have to decide whether a given activity should be dealt with in-house or if they should have a certain number of tasks or functions carried out by outside firms. This issue has become increasingly thorny and crucial as a result of the trend towards what is termed reengineering[2], a process set up to

1. M. Patry, To Do it, or to Have it Done: the Future of Organization Economy, CIRANO-HEC, Montreal, 2000.

2. M. Hammer and J. Champy, *Reengineering the Corporation: a Manifesto for Business Revolution*, Harper Collins Publishers, New York, 1993.

adapt the structures of firms in order to improve their performance within the constricting context of hypercompetition.

Although it is sometimes reduced to simplistic recipes or a merely fashionable concept, the principle of reengineering[1] is interesting, as it consists in starting from scratch to find solutions to complex problems. This is admittedly not a wholly recent intellectual process. As long ago as the 14th century, the Latin expression *tabula rasa* (literally a smooth or blank tablet), denoting an Aristotelian principle taken up in the 17th century by John Locke, to explain the origin of thought and representation in humankind. Reengineering is in fact a kind of state of mind forming a prerequisite for diagnosis and the formulation of new solutions. It rejects the traditional boundaries separating functions and departments within the company, making it possible to reconstruct the production processes at a fundamental level, in order to reduce costs and execution times as well as improving quality.

Thanks to reengineering, it is possible to introduce more horizontal than vertical relationships into companies, more delegation and less centralization, a constant learning process and an increasing role for operatives as opposed to members of the executive. This way of treating problems is a response to the new challenges that have emerged over the past few years. In modern companies, it is no longer possible to pursue their quest for progress on the margins, since such a method is only valid in a stable environment. When the environment alters to a greater or lesser extent, as is happening today, it is necessary to question the paradigms that served as a basis in the past when seeking to maintain or improve performance.

The return to core business is thus an application of this method, as it questions the traditional organization of firms, revising everything from A to Z. Over the last few years, this attempt at streamlining activities in order to concentrate on the companies' strong points (its basic skills) and avoid fragmentation into different fields

---

1. Grammatically speaking, the term "reengineering" is what is called a "derivative", meaning that a new lexical unit is created by adding a dependent element – an "affix", more precisely in this case a prefix – to an existing word. The prefix *re-* marks the repetition of an action, though it may also denote a return to a former state. "Reengineering" thus has a twofold meaning, in that it designates a continuous, repetitive process and an attitude that makes it possible to see situations in a different light by tackling the problem at its source.

has become an almost universal watchword. This is why many companies, in order to become stronger, have abandoned their so-called "peripheral" operations and have subcontracted or outsourced them, having them carried out by other firms, thus devoting their energies to their core business, the field in which their true expertise lies.

The theories on expertise traditionally make a distinction between different types of skills: individual and collective, explicit and implicit, tangible and intangible, cognitive and behavioral, and technological and organizational. Knowledge, know-how and behavior are thus the three dimensions affording better understanding of what an organization is capable of. This balance is complex, but a company's competitiveness is always based on its core skills.

Although this model is universally recognized, it is worth considering whether the very notion of "core business" is as important today as in the past. In a context of constant evolution such as the one we are experiencing today, the priorities established at a given time cannot be maintained indefinitely for ever-changing activities. For example, S. Tchuruk, CEO of Alcatel, asserted in 1997 that the manufacture of mobile telephones was a strategic choice for his company, yet four years later (probably for these same reasons), he sold this branch to the Singaporean outsourcing giant Flextronics.

The distribution of competences, making the distinction between the fundamental skills and the rest, leads to an oversimplification of the company. While the research on this subject carried out by Prahalad and Hamel[1] makes a useful contribution, this reasoning should not be taken too far, since the results may finally be absurd. The key, or fundamental, skill of Tiger Woods is obviously golf, but this great sportsman also earns an extremely high income from advertising contracts. Since in his particular situation advertising is clearly not a fundamental activity, should he give it up or outsource it? The distinction between what is fundamental and what is not evidently does not provide a basis for a decision on outsourcing.

Recourse to outside service providers began with so-called minor or subsidiary functions (janitor services, staff catering, cleaning, etc.) before developing significantly. Increasingly specific functions were then entrusted to outside service providers such as the management of IT systems, accounting, staff recruitment and advertising.

---

1. G. Hamel and C. Prahalad, "The Core Competence of the Corporation", *Harvard Business Review*, n° 68, 1990.

At present, as most studies show, the number of functions sub-contracted or outsourced is rising constantly. The latest survey by Ernst and Young, carried out in 2003[1], shows that in France, for example, companies outsource an average of four and a half functions, and that this new form of production organization is used by 62% of companies, the following being at the top of the ranking:
  – distribution, logistics and transport (51%);
  – support services such as property management, catering and document management (49%);
  – IT and telecommunications (48%).

It must be added that the number of functions carried out outside the company is increasing constantly. It should not however be forgotten that France has not made great progress in this field compared to such countries as the United Kingdom, where this method of production organization has been widely applied for a long time.

Subcontracting: no Recent Invention

Subcontracting is an age-old practice. It emerged at the beginning of the merchant economy in the Middle Ages, long before the industrial era. Cathedral builders themselves had recourse to the services of sculptors, carpenters, stonemasons and their companion trades. However, it developed considerably with the expansion of exchanges during the 19th century. For example, the wool producers in northern France had their wool washed in Verviers in eastern Belgium, then in Mazamet in southern France.

Since the Second World War, subcontracting has altered with the sizes of the markets, automation and the standardization of procedures. As the production processes became more and more complex, in an effort to simplify their functioning, companies now no longer subcontract individual elements or sets of elements, but complete functions. It may even be said that recourse to outside service providers is becoming a necessity if companies wish to maintain a certain competitive edge.

---

1. Ernst and Young, *Baromètre, Outsourcing 2003, pratiques et tendances de l'externalisation en France*, 2003 (Barometer, Outsourcing 2003, outsourcing practices and trends in France). This survey was carried out between May 26 and June 23, 2003, among 220 general, administrative or financial managers of whom 47% work in industry, 17% in banking and insurance, 13% in distribution and trade, and 23% in other sectors.

Generally speaking, a company never manufactures all the products it needs to ensure its own production; apart from raw materials, it purchases or subcontracts many of the factors it uses.

In the case of a simple purchase, the specifications of products available on the market correspond to its needs, and there is no advantage (quality, cost, etc.) to be drawn from internal production.

In the second case – subcontracting – the company defines its specifications for aspects which are dealt with by suppliers who are called in on request.

Consequently, subcontracting consists in using resources outside the company to improve production usually carried out by internal resources through internal coordination. This practice, through which a company entrusts its major functions to specialized, efficient suppliers, may then lead to partnerships in value enhancement.

This recourse to outside services can take several forms according to the circumstances and motivations of the principal; it is then known as capacity or specialty subcontracting.

– *Capacity subcontracting* occurs when the company considers it unprofitable to acquire extra resources in terms of machinery or labor force that would subsequently be only partly used. In this perspective the main company then takes on another company or shares the extra operations among several companies.

This extra workload may be an exception, implying for the principal an adjustment of capacity, either when there is a sharp or unforeseen increase in orders or in the event of a temporary malfunction in the company's materials, for example a breakdown. Airlines often use this type of subcontracting, by renting aircraft from rival companies to deal with peaks in traffic.

– *Structural subcontracting* arises from another type of decision and involves many more firms. The company's management may voluntarily postpone investments likely to increase its production capacity because the quantities to be produced do not justify it or because production processes are not yet stabilized. Subcontracting enables it, with no financial risk, to expect that the quantities to be produced will be sufficient to make a given integrated production tool profitable. This type of outsourcing is also used when the principal's activity fluctuates, for example seasonally, and thus makes it possible to organize production capacity to respond to peaks in the workload.

– *Specialty subcontracting* is different, being used when the company considers it does not have the technical expertise or specialized equipment required for the execution of a certain type of task. In this case, the principal calls upon techniques or expertise it does not have or that it cannot acquire in an economically viable way. In this case, the subcontractor is often entrusted with a role directly connected to the design of the product itself. Relations between the two partners are then based not on subordination but on equality and reciprocal obligations.

Thus, since the very origins of companies, some of the products and factors they need to ensure smooth operations are provided by the market, i.e. by other companies. However, a noteworthy development has emerged over the past few years, for this recourse to outside service providers, formerly limited to parts or components of the manufactured products, has extended to complete functions.

Consequently, beyond the classic relationships between principals and subcontractors, more complex, long-term relationships have developed, surpassing those traditionally found in subcontracting arrangements.

Outsourcing: an Innovation!

Should an insurance company have its own IT department or should it call upon an outside service provider specialized in facilities management, to carry out this function? What led Siemens, the major German industrial group, to entrust part of its logistics and spare-parts management to the *Bundespost*, the German national postal service? Why did the Unilever Group choose British Telecom (BT) to set up and manage all its land and mobile telephone installations all over the world? These are only a few examples.

Over the last few years, recourse to the market has become increasingly frequent, and the range of functions carried out outside the company has considerably broadened. Simple traditional subcontracting has gradually given way to a new conception of the phenomenon known as outsourcing.

Outsourcing must be distinguished from subcontracting, as the term outsourcing implies that the activity entrusted to an outside agency formerly existed within the company, which is generally not the case for subcontracting.

The most commonly accepted definition of outsourcing is as follows: "Outsourcing, in its most basic form, can be conceived of as the purchase of a good or service that was previously provided internally... It now represents a significant transfer of assets, leases and staff to a vendor that assumes profit and loss responsibility"[1].

For Barthélemy[2], this traditional definition does not take into account a fundamental aspect, the wish of the outsourcing company to retain control over the management of the resources it entrusts to outside service providers. Thus he suggests reformulating the definition in two parts:

– outsourcing consists in the transfer of ownership of all or part of an activity formerly carried out internally and may sometimes involve the transfer of staff;

– outsourcing is based on a long- or short-term contract according to the classic or strategic nature of the activity being outsourced. It is also based on organizational arrangements. The service provider is supposed to replace the internal services of the outsourcing company, which implies major changes at an organizational level. In the event of "total" outsourcing, only the management of the activity remains internal, as it is management that determines future needs.

More generally, it may be said that outsourcing is a strategic decision for a company trying to determine whether it should carry out a given operation itself or have recourse to an outside service provider. It should also be pointed out that the dividing line between internal and external aspects of a production system is not intangible and may be adjusted according to the firm's long-term strategy.

As seen above, companies have always concluded contracts for carrying out certain specific tasks or to cope with peaks in their workload. They have thus forged special links with firms whose expertise rounds off their own. However, the difference between simply using complementary resources and outsourcing is that the latter often involves major structural changes in certain operations, or even in the company as a whole.

Today, outsourcing is rightly considered to be a strategic decision, since it consists in having activities essential to the function-

---

1. M. Lacity and R. Hirschheim, "The Information Systems Outsourcing Bandwagon", *Sloan Management Review*, Fall 1993, pp. 13-25.

2. J. Barthélemy, "La dimension contractuelle de l'outsourcing: analyse théorique et étude de quinze cas informatiques français" (The contractual dimension of outsourcing: theoretical analysis and study of fifteen IT cases in France), 7th international conference on strategic management, Louvain-la-Neuve, Belgium, May 27-29, 1998.

ing of the firm itself carried out outside the company. Unlike the case of subcontracting, its initial purpose is no longer merely to reduce costs. Outsourcing is becoming a true management method, as stated in 1996 by the Outsourcing Institute: "The use of outsourcing as a management tool by today's organization has evolved beyond being a tactical measure to become a strategic initiative"[1]. In fact, outsourcing means purchasing results rather than means from a supplier who is also responsible for managing the process leading up to the expected results.

Outsourcing is also distinct from simple subcontracting because it encompasses a particularly broad field, in fact concerning most according to Porter's definition:
- infrastructure;
- human resources management;
- technological development;
- supplies;
- information and communication technology[2].

They may even bear on primary activities such as after-sales service or transport, which both contribute to value creation in their own ways.

A Question of Strategy

Outsourcing is part of the strategy of any company. It constitutes a real decision-making process going far beyond mere technical or financial choices.

Thanks to the research carried out by Simon[3] (Nobel Prize 1970), it is possible to define three key phases in the decision-making process, by adopting a psycho-sociological approach:
- "intelligence": before making a decision, it is necessary to detect and identify the problem to be solved (identification);
- "modeling": once the problem has been isolated, it must be specified and its contours delineated, a process that includes determining its structure and establishing the analogies with problems solved previously;

---

1. The Outsourcing Institute is a professional association with almost 30,000 members, set up some ten years ago.

2. *Op. cit.*

3. H. Simon, *The New Science of Management Decision*, Harper & Row, New York, 1960.

The Difference between Subcontracting and Outsourcing[a]

Take the example of two companies operating in the same sector that decide to take part in a trade fair. Each of the companies builds a stand to present its offer and its products.

– The first traditionally manages the building of its stand, designating an internal project manager in charge of coordinating the various agents involved. The project manager chooses an architect to design the stand and subcontracts a large number of tasks: blueprints, installation, electricity supply, choice of furniture, etc.

– The second decides to outsource the management of the entire project. To do so, it signs a contract with a single agency dealing with both design and installation. The agency, as it is well acquainted with all those involved in the project, can negotiate certain advantages thanks to its experience in the field, which advantages are passed on to the final client.

– The results are obvious. In the first instance, adding up all the costs incurred through the various transactions, as well as the labor time spent internally, the total cost of the stand reaches EUR 6 million. In the second, the company having delegated the project from beginning to end, i.e. outsourced, gave the outside agency a budget of EUR 2 million, one third of the other's budget, and in addition enjoyed greater flexibility.

a. Ernst and Young, *Barometer, Outsourcing 2002*, (Barometer, Outsourcing 2002).

– "choice": the stage leading to the proposal of a solution.

This approach, known as the IMC model, has been developed considerably, and two points require some clarification.

– First, the relative importance of each of these stages is variable according to the decision at hand. In some cases, only the choice counts; in others, the intelligence phase proves to be essential. For example, to meet increased demand, the most important factor is to determine by how much production should be increased. In contrast, to launch a new product within three years, an attempt must first be made to forecast the major qualitative and quantitative curves in demand.

– Second, the phenomenon of feedback is central. The decision-making process does not always follow a linear route from intelligence to choice. A looping progression often illustrates the need to return to a previous stage. For example, it may be concluded that it is impossible to provide a solution to a problem because of erroneous or incomplete identification. If failure is noted as the choice is being made, the intelligence phase needs to be reviewed.

The decision to outsource some corporate duties is perfectly coherent with this type of approach, since it is an important decision forming part of a rational approach that has little to do with chance but must be integrated into the company's strategy.

In economic and managerial literature, there are several typologies of decision-making processes, differentiated by the criteria chosen to distinguish them. However, it is always the first method of classification used historically that is the best known and the most widely used. This method is based on the importance given to the consequences of the decisions made.

This method was first applied to warfare and was formalized, in particular by Carl von Clausewitz[1] as long ago as 1832. It distinguishes three main levels, which are, in decreasing order of importance:

- *the strategic level*: the necessity of engaging in combat;
- *the tactical level*: the choice of battle plan;
- *the operational level*: the execution of the battle plan in the field.

This hierarchy of decisions is still used in the military field, but the significance of the levels has changed with technical progress. The distinction, common nowadays, between tactical nuclear weapons and strategic nuclear weapons, is an illustration of this semantic transformation[2].

The theory of organizations has taken up this classification of decisions by level, but it occasionally uses rather less warlike vocabulary. The three levels are then labeled as follows:

- *planning* (or *strategic planning*): this is the development of the major objectives of the organization (development lines) to which it commits itself in the future;
- *steering*: this consists in defining quantitatively and qualitatively the means to be deployed in order to attain the objectives;
- *regulation*: this is the material deployment of these means, with monitoring of results and correction of disparities in relation to forecasts.

---

1. C. von Clausewitz, *Vom Kriege*, 1832, translated as *On War*.

2. Tactical weapons are those of the battlefield, and as such are relatively short-range. Strategic weapons are long-range, and are more often intended to destroy economic or purely civilian targets.

Thus, the choice of producing internally is an *operational* decision relating to *regulation*, and in this case the means must be materially deployed in the field in order to attain the objectives. However, the decision to subcontract is a *tactical* decision relating to *steering*, since it requires deciding on a battle plan and choosing the nature of means to be deployed. Finally, the decision to outsource is a *strategic* decision relating to *planning*, as it involves defining the objectives to which the company commits itself in the future.

Nor should it be forgotten that for outsourcing to be successful, the structural forms must be appropriate and efficient. The question of the efficiency of the structures is essential. It is a complex issue as it involves determining the criteria the organization must satisfy in order for the performance of the company to be as profitable as possible, given the constraints imposed by the environment. A fundamental contribution on this point was made several years ago by Ansoff and Brandenburg[1]. These authors isolated, within the company, two major subsystems: the logistics subsystem and the management subsystem.

– The logistics subsystem groups together all activities linked to the transformation of resources acquired by the company into products intended for sale. It goes from research and development to after-sales service, and corresponds to production activities in the broad sense of the term[2].

– The management subsystem is made up of all the administration and monitoring mechanisms within the company.

These processes are traditionally structured according to their levels and the methods used. The authors then propose four criteria making it possible to evaluate the various aspects of efficiency of a mode of internal organization.

Efficiency in stasis corresponds to cases in which the nature and level of the company's activities do not change. The company must be able to produce at the lowest possible cost, and must thus seek to take the greatest possible advantage of potential economies of scale. However, the few decisions that have to be taken are repetitive. The management subsystem may, however, be only slightly developed.

---

1. H. Ansoff and R. Brandenburg, "A Language for Organization Design", *Management Science*, August 1971.

2. The logistics subsystem closely resembles the primary activities as defined by Porter (1985).

Operational flexibility is the aptitude of a company to modify rapidly and at low cost its production levels. The logistics system, along with part of the management system, must be decentralized to reduce delays in reaction to changes in the environment.

Strategic flexibility lies in the ability to adapt the range of products at very short notice. To do so, it is necessary to carry out a systematic analysis of the environment, including technology intelligence. The production mechanisms must also be designed to manufacture old and new products simultaneously, and the first are generally only gradually replaced by the second.

Structural flexibility is shown by the company's ability to modify its own internal organization. This presupposes great flexibility in the workforce and in equipment, which is rare, and great receptivity to new ideas, which is even less common.

It is obvious that working towards efficiency according to the organizational modes described above must in the first, less complex, cases – efficiency in stasis and operational flexibility – fall back on subcontracting; in the two other cases, namely strategic flexibility and structural flexibility, companies will have recourse to outsourcing.

Why Outsource?

Economic theory has never examined outsourcing closely, as noted by Lei and Hitt[1]. Yet as observed above, it is a vital question.

The reasons compelling a company to outsource are many and varied. If variations in workload – which are simply dealt with through subcontracting – are excluded, there remain two types of managerial motivation, strategic and financial, leading to decisions to outsource.

There are many strategic motives leading a company to turn to outside service providers for the accomplishment of certain tasks, but the following are the three main reasons:

– Seeking know-how that the company does not possess and that others master more effectively. As specialized service providers possess greater expertise than is generally found in the internal departments of a company, outsourcing makes it possible to keep up with technical progress.

---

1. D. Lei and M. Hitt, "Strategic Restructuring and Outsourcing: the Effects of Mergers and Acquisitions and LBOs on Building Firm Skills and Capabilities", *Journal of Management*, 1995, 21, 5, pp. 835-859.

– Refusing to invest, either because the production levels are too low or because the market progress forecasts are not accurate enough.

– Wishing to galvanize subsidiaries or specific branches by setting them in competition with outside service providers.

The move toward outsourcing also has financial motivations, and from this point of view two major reasons are frequently given to justify choosing this option.

– Seeking lower costs, either because the outside company dealing with production is located in a country or region where direct labor costs are particularly low, or because the outside company, by virtue of its specialization, has greater productivity thanks to more profitable use of its equipment or greater mastery of the technology. However, as will be explored below, if only the criterion of cost is applied, financial logic would dictate increasing outsourcing to a probably excessive degree.

– Effective cash-flow management may also be an argument in favor of outsourcing, since in this case, instead of paying labor costs regularly, for example at the end of each month, the principal (i.e. the company outsourcing its activity) settles these costs after a certain lapse of time. Furthermore, it should be added that in the event of a decrease in production, when an activity is outsourced the company is not concerned with job losses and thus does not have to bear any costs – human, social or financial – relating to redundancies. Of course, it is often some combination of the above.

In fact, the major risk in the event of ill-prepared outsourcing is to an extent the loss of a certain cohesion within the company that turns to outside service providers. This is why, in such cases, it is necessary to rethink regularly human resources management and to modify the organization of the company, since recourse to an outside supplier can alter or break up the classic relationship one has to one's work, in particular the twin principles of commitment and job security, which form the cornerstone of salaried employment.

Can Everything be Outsourced?

Since the late 1980s, companies have been swept along in a vast movement encouraging them to return to "their" core businesses. It is a question of streamlining management by trimming down companies and by limiting the diversity of their activities, at the same time taking advantage of increased division of labor. This last point, according to the principles of classic economic analysis, makes it possible to increase productivity.

In their famous article, Quinn and Hilmer[1] show that all activities can be outsourced, even those that are traditionally part of the company, with the exception of those at the heart of its operations. In their view, every company should concentrate on a limited number of "core competencies" for which it may obtain or maintain a competitive edge.

They point out that one essential rule must be observed at all times: they must painstakingly control their transaction costs, for the markets on which the outside service providers operate are not always efficient or trustworthy, and the predicted costs may be higher than expected. They add that "the issue is less whether to make or buy an activity than it is how to structure... external sourcing on an optimal basis."

It is clearly difficult to bring together all the parameters that should be taken into account before deciding to outsource. This is why Gordon, Vollman and Heikkilä[2] suggest grouping competencies together into five major categories for a better grasp of their roles within the company.

– *Specific* competencies: the most important competencies in any given company, for example engines at Renault and software at Microsoft.

– *Fundamental* competencies: the activities necessary for the running of the company, such as the quality of management processes and ISO certification.

– *Ricochet* competencies: competencies making it possible to make a profit in a secondary activity thanks to a specific skill (for example, the case of Tiger Woods, as seen above, when performing advertising contracts).

– *Protection* competencies: those arising from activities that may lead to serious malfunctions if poorly managed.

– *Parasite* competencies: activities carried out internally that lead to a waste of resources.

---

1. J. Quinn and F. Hilmer, "Strategic Outsourcing", *Sloan Management Review*, Summer 1994.

2. Three professors at the Institute for Management Development (IMD), the Lausanne Business School, Switzerland. "Penser clairement l'externalisation" in *L'art de l'entreprise globale* (Clear Thinking on Outsourcing in the Art of General Management), Les Échos, 1998.

For these three authors, this model can only be dynamic, as the different activities can change category over the course of time. A *fundamental* activity may become a *parasite* depending on how the environment changes. When a western company, for example, sets up in a developing country such as China, it is almost compelled to produce internally in the absence of reliable suppliers. However, in time, competent suppliers eventually come into existence, which soon encourages these expatriate companies to outsource certain operations that had become parasites.

Thus, on the basis of this model, it is possible to determine what should be outsourced and what should not. It is obvious that this is necessarily the case for all the *parasite* competencies and to a certain extent for the *fundamental* and *protection* competencies. Ricochet competencies may also be outsourced, provided the profits derived from this type of competency do in fact fall to the company.

Given its importance and complexity, it is clear that outsourcing is an issue to be dealt with by general management. General management must make the decisions in this respect, after, naturally, examination of the case by the management of the individual activity.

In fact, all competencies, whatever their nature, contribute to building up specific competencies which are not outsourced, but all of them may evolve and transform over time. Nevertheless, the authors of this model regret that so few companies have well-defined methods or policies for making outsourcing decisions. This is a grave omission when all the implications such a decision can have on the functioning of a company are taken into consideration.

Many studies have shown that before deciding to outsource a function or not, it is vital to examine the case upstream from all angles, so as to prevent the company from losing its key competencies, in a word, its very substance. Thus, it is always important to bear in mind that any outsourcing decision includes a number of risk of which the company should be aware as well as the magnitude of those risks.

Since a major objective of company organization is the constant striving for flexibility and adaptability, it can more generally be observed that firms seek to decentralize the decision-making process more and more and develop profit centers operating in networks. The three basic principles that have long been adhered to in the design of the production process – unity of time, unity of place and unity of action – thus give a comfortable margin to organizations operating both with many internal agents and external partners.

Most Frequently Outsourced Primary and Secondary Functions

Seven categories of functions are often outsourced, and within these major activities can be found over thirty specific functions that are commonly executed outside the company.

1. Production
- Research and development
- Production of goods
- Production of services
- Maintenance
- Packaging

2. Distribution, Logistics and Transport
- Storage and shipping
- Transport
- Conveyance and distribution
- Vehicle fleet

3. Computing and Telecommunications
- Office management
- Network and server management
- Soft- and hardware maintenance
- Communications management

4. Human Resources
- Training
- Recruitment
- Pay
- Personnel administration

5. Administration and Finance
- Legal, tax and insurance matters
- Accounting
- Internal audit
- Purchasing management
- Sales management
- Share and asset management
- Cash flow management

6. Marketing and Communication
- Customer relations (call centers)
- External communication (press and public relations)

7. General Services
- Catering
- Property management
- Caretaking, security and cleaning
- Documentation management (mail, archives)
- Office supplies (e-procurement)
- Teleservices, reception and secretarial services

The age when all companies wanted to do everything themselves is now over; the vertical integration that made it possible for years to obtain stricter standards of quality and avoid suppliers' profit margins is no longer valid. In all countries and in all companies, there has been a growth in the number of contractualization proposals for all functions: in production with true outsourcing, in sales with franchises and in finance with leasing, etc.

Outsourcing in Figures

The economic weight of outsourcing is growing continuously. It is now a production method affecting not only large corporations but also small and medium-sized companies as well as entities within the public sector.

Ernst and Young's 2003 study on outsourcing in France[1] confirms the trends that had been observed in previous years, and highlights four major phenomena:

– The managers who responded are clearly aware of outsourcing and are better able to define it, most often assimilating it to the delegation of a function. Furthermore, the proportion of companies resorting to outsourcing is now 62%, as opposed to 60% in 1999.

– The number of outsourced functions is growing steadily, from an average of two in 1999 to four and a half today. In addition, over 92% of companies consider that in the long run the scope of outsourced functions will not decrease; on the contrary, the managers responding believed it would continue to rise, or at worst remain stable.

– In the future, i.e. in the next two years, a third of the companies are considering outsourcing new functions.

– Finally, and this is perhaps the most important point, the satisfaction rate with regard to outsourcing is particularly high, at over 90%.

While there are certain barriers to outsourcing, in particular the fear of losing control over the functions entrusted to other companies, it is nevertheless a worldwide phenomenon, spreading steadily whatever the size of the company. In the United States, for example:

– 60% of companies with fewer than 500 employees will be spending between one and five million dollars on outsourced activities in the next twelve months[2].

---

1. *Op. cit.*
2. Source: The Outsourcing Institute, 2003.

– The outsourced documentation market, growing at a rate of 12% a year, should amount to 50 billion dollars in 2005, as opposed to 27.8 billion in 2000[1].

– Since 1989, outsourced IT expenditure has risen by an average of 25% a year, and according to the US Department of Commerce should reach 150 billion dollars in 2003.

– Of the 500 billion dollars generated by the American automobile industry, external suppliers now account for almost two thirds.

There are countless examples, for it now applies to all companies. However, while the private sector is adopting this organizational method, how is it affecting the public sector?

In local authorities such as city halls, certain functions have been outsourced for a long time: waste collection, park management, school catering and cleaning, etc. Today, the new development is that these authorities are outsourcing new, more "noble" functions such as IT management, vehicle fleet management and staff training.

However, outsourcing policies are still relatively rare in central administrations. The French Defense Ministry did nonetheless set an example when, in 2002, it allocated EUR 533 million – 17% of its operating budget – to outsourcing, and other ministries will be following suit over the next few years. It is much the same elsewhere in the world. For example, the US Army has chosen to outsource its healthcare services, entrusting them to private firms.

While preparing the 2004 budget, the French Prime Minister asserted that the state had to "refocus onto its core activities" and that "certain tasks could be delegated". In less than three years, outsourcing has become standard practice for public authorities, and is even at the heart of state reform.

Using the Ernst and Young survey of France[2], it is possible to group companies together, according to their outsourcing practices, into four categories:

– The converts (32%): these outsource almost six different functions and wish to go still further over the next two years.

– The believers (30%): these outsource one to four functions and intend to develop this practice over the next few months.

– The hesitators (8%): for the moment, these outsource none of their functions, but plan to do so over the next two years.

---

1. Source: CAP Ventures, February 2002.
2. *Op. cit.*

– The opponents (30%): these do not outsource and have no intention of doing so in the short term.

As can be noted, over two thirds of companies have incorporated this management method into their operations and fully intend to develop it further.

When and How to Outsource

According to J.C. Jarillo[1], all industrial and service firms sooner or later have to make the currently classic choice of "doing it" or "having it done" for many of their activities.

In the case of the integration of an activity, the company has to bear internal costs (IC), including both labor costs and capital expenditure.

In the case of outsourcing, i.e. "having it done", the company has to take into account both acquisition costs (AC) and transaction costs (TC), bringing total costs to AC + CT. Acquisition costs include the cost of the product or activity carried out externally, and transaction costs cover the expenditure necessary for obtaining information and sealing the outsourcing agreement by contract.

It is obvious that the activity will be carried out internally when AC + TC > IC; the same is true even when AC < IC.

On the other hand, when AC + TC < IC, the company benefits from opting for outsourcing, thus obtaining from suppliers skills that could only be produced internally at high cost.

Generally, the expected profit from outsourcing amounts to average savings of some 15 to 30%, but as seen above, outsourcing cannot be reduced to the level of a mere "beauty contest", the winner being the one making the most attractive offer. Outsourcing involves real commitment over several years (5 to 10), and requires consideration of many parameters just as important as cost-effectiveness, for example the quality of the equipment used and production processes.

In addition, a follow-up procedure must be set up for each outsourcing operation. This is an essential factor, even if little research has been carried out on the subject. Consultancies do offer various formulae that are little more than common-sense recommendations, such as refusing model contracts, taking expert advice before

---

1. "On Strategic Networks", *Strategic Management Journal*, 1988.

making a decision and carrying out trial runs. The most interesting publications on follow-up procedures concern the very nature of the contracts governing any outsourcing operation, which can be grouped together into two categories:

– short-term contracts essentially intended to govern the company's low-risk or non-strategic activities;

– long-term contacts covering sensitive or strategic services that move beyond mere financial considerations to integrate relationship- and trust-building provisions.

A further point to be borne in mind is that outsourcing, as seen above, is an intermediate form of governance between the market and internal organizations. As it is generally based on complex long-term contracts, it requires special monitoring. The external service provider to whom this type of operation is entrusted must be assessed on several points: speed, cost, quality of work, team turnover, working environment and staff training. Naturally, in order to proceed with such an assessment, it is vital to call in experts able to look beyond mere questions of price control and cost.

Purchasing Managers, to whom this responsibility often falls, can no longer be restricted to their roles of merely dealing with order books. They must be acquainted not only with the products but also with the different businesses, thus being in a position to submit proposals to the CEO. In industry, they are often referred to as "Purchasing Engineers".

Ultimately, outsourcing most often brings about major organizational changes. It affects the functioning of a company at three main levels:

– first, it leads to the creation of particular entities responsible for monitoring outside service providers;

– then, it modifies the management role for the activity resorting to outsourcing, turning from a hierarchical entity into a steering and monitoring entity;

– finally, it entails reconsideration of the role of the outside service provider, as it is no longer a mere subcontractor but a genuine partner integrated into the organization.

For J.B. Quinn, the outsourcing company is the first step towards a modular company or network focusing on its core competencies and having the rest done externally[1].

---

1. J.B. Quinn, *The Intelligent Enterprise: a Knowledge and Service-Based Paradigm for the Industry*, New York, The Free Press, 1992.

The Case of Nortel Networks

The Canadian company Nortel, one of the largest telecommunications equipment manufacturers in the world, announced in late January 2004 that it was to transfer to Singaporean company Flextronics all its remaining production activities, in particular its factories in Canada, Brazil, Northern Ireland and France.

Nortel's management indicated that it wished to concentrate on new products and complex multi-technology equipment. This outsourcing process consisted in transferring manufacturing assets and stock worth over 500 million dollars against the backdrop of the "factory-free" company, as the Canadian manufacturer had already outsourced 85% of its production units.

This strategy enabled Nortel to gain access to the best production technologies and to react swiftly to the changing needs of the market.

For some analysts, while the advantages are obvious, there is nonetheless the risk of a split between developing and perfecting equipment. It was this very risk that led its principal competitor, German firm Siemens, to decide not to outsource everything in order to retain a certain degree of control over production.

Advantages, Disadvantages and Barriers

According to Ernst and Young[1], companies consider that outsourcing provides many advantages, which can be grouped together into four categories:

– Finding the best price and the greatest level of effectiveness is considered to be the main advantage of outsourcing by over 54% of companies, compared to 41% two years ago.

– Obtaining greater quality and more competencies is the second advantage cited by 48% of companies. It must be added that many firms consider that the favorable cost/effectiveness ratio is a means not only of reducing variable costs but also their standing charges, resulting in an economy of scale.

– In third place come flexibility and simplicity. However, the wish to obtain this type of advantage, sought by 46% of companies, has been steadily increasing in the last few years.

---

1. *Op. cit.*

– Finally, for a growing number of companies (more than one in five), outsourcing is considered a means of instituting a more effective mode of organization.

However, for companies having opted for outsourcing, all is not necessarily rosy. There are also a number of disadvantages that may, if they are not taken into account, call into question the positive effects of the choices made or slow down the development of this new mode of organization. Five disadvantages are often cited:

1. Loss of control over the function that it has been decided to outsource, a disadvantage for 46% of the companies surveyed.

2. The low quality of services obtained from outside service providers, cited by 33% of companies.

3. The cost of the outsourced activity, considered to be too high by 26% of companies.

4. Human problems arising from outsourcing, troublesome for 24% of companies.

5. Finally, the loss of expertise and competencies is a disadvantage for 21% of respondents.

Nevertheless, all these disadvantages have little consequence on the choices companies make, as 77% of the companies continued their outsourcing operations in 2003.

Outsourcing in France is far from having reached its apogee. It should continue to grow over the next few years, and may even double by 2007. There is a similar trend in all the industrialized countries.

The quest for optimum flexibility so as to be able to adapt to an increasingly uncertain and complex world encourages companies not only to manage better, but also to manage swiftly and differently. This forces them to develop their functioning and organization in new ways, giving greater and greater importance to the new concepts used in network or virtual companies. To reach such an objective, managing costs is not enough; it is also necessary to risk outsourcing value-generating functions for which the company has no decisive advantage. There subsists a certain squeamishness with regard to change, and some psychological obstacles are always tenacious. For the most part, they consist of cultural barriers, in particular the desire to control everything, which obviously leads to a serious reluctance to entrust part of the work to third parties.

It is now clear that outsourcing has achieved legitimacy, as it meets a specific need and furthermore makes it possible to come close to the dream of all managers, that of building up an ideal organization.

Occupational Hazards

Given its importance in both economic and organizational terms, it is clear that any outsourcing process involves a number of risks. These risks are often underestimated or veiled by the importance given to the financial benefits expected from this new production method[1].

– The first type of risk concerns the strategic approach to activities, more specifically the choice of the function to be outsourced. Certain functions may be considered non-strategic at one given moment then finally become strategic following market developments. Thus, for example, logistics[2] may become a strategic function rather than a mere technical activity. Furthermore, outsourcing occasionally involves an irrevocable loss of expertise, since the new production method, accompanied by a transfer of equipment and/or staff, leads to a loss of individual, collective and organizational competencies. The quest for short-term effectiveness may lead to long-term vulnerability.

– Second, there are risks connected to the control of the concern itself. Outsourcing is not the same as downsizing, the latter consisting in the simple transfer of an activity to another company, since the relationship between a buyer and a seller comes to an end once the sale is made, whereas in outsourcing, the relationships between firms subsist over time with some form of interdependency emerging. For example, many companies that have entrusted all their computing systems to outside agencies as part of facilities management agreements have become dependent on these agencies. These close links lead to very high switching costs when the company wishes to call upon other suppliers, and this may make reintegration impossible. It is important to bear service quality in mind dur-

---

1. F. Arfaoui, G. Bohbot and B. N'Gazo (Price Waterhouse Coopers), "Les risques de la stratégie d'externalisation" (The Risks Inherent to Outsourcing Strategy), *Les Échos*, October 2000.

2. Logistics is a function grouping together all the flows toward the customer (finished products, spare parts), transferred between or within production units (half-finished products, products at intermediate stages) and finally received from suppliers (raw materials, components).

ing monitoring. Outsourced activities do not always meet expectations quality-wise, and it was precisely this concern that prompted the Novotel hotel chain to reintegrate its cleaning operations, taking the opportunity to turn a cost item into a vector of added value.

– The third risk involves controlling profitability. While outsourcing makes it possible to reduce "visible" costs perceptibly, it also leads to certain "hidden" costs, generated by the control and supervision of the service provider's actions. Occasionally, the service provider is unable to meet the initially given specifications. Furthermore, there is always a risk of failure on the part of the service provider for technical, economic or financial reasons, and the consequences of this are serious since they may lead to the entire operation coming to a standstill.

– Finally, there is a risk connected to staffing, particularly when posts are transferred or terminated. Latent or overt industrial disputes can arise. Therefore the human dimension must always be taken into account in any outsourcing process. This must be based on open information flow and clear communication alongside requalification measures and skill management.

It is however possible to control or to limit outsourcing risks by making all decision in this area part of a medium- or long-term prospective process, meaning that the advantages expected in the short term, such as cost reduction, must not hide the effects of outsourcing on all the companies activities and thus on the value chain.

In the modern environment, the more competition develops, the more it is necessary to find solutions in external cooperation. These responses to the challenges companies have to face go far beyond subcontracting and even outsourcing. New arrangements which go even further recommending long-term cooperation solutions, are becoming necessary. They are essential factors in modern management and may be classified under the general heading of "Laborgistics®".

CHAPTER 4 :

Laborgistics®

As Drucker recalls[1], a century ago the vast majority of the population in industrialized countries were manual workers, mostly in agriculture or crafts, with a minority in industry. Fifty years later, the proportion of manual workers had fallen by a half in the United States, with blue-collar workers accounting for 35% of the active population. Today, manual workers only account for 25% of workers in the United States, and blue-collar workers no more than 15% of the working population. Over the past few years, all the industrialized countries, such as the United Kingdom, Japan, Germany and France, have been developing in the same way. In other words, we have now entered a phase where the economy is based on services, a world revolving around "knowledge workers", as Drucker and Machlup[2] put it, and these new workers have transformed not only society but also the way businesses are managed.

A remarkable feature of the industrial revolution was the emergence, thanks to the use of mechanical machines, of large-scale production. The period we are in now is markedly different because of the greater importance of intangible assets and products. The production structure, as well as the nature of production processes, is changing. The importance of physical goods and equipment is gradually decreasing in relation to that of intangible services and assets. The most visible and best-known aspect of this phenomenon

---

1. P. Drucker, *Managing in the Next Society*, Truman Talley Books, 2002.
2. Fritz Machlup (1902-1983), an American economist of Austrian descent.

What is a Service?

A service-based activity is essentially characterized by the placing at the client's disposal of technical or intellectual skills. It cannot be qualified merely by the characteristics of an intangible good acquired by the customer. In its broadest sense, the notion of service encompasses a vast range of activities, from transport, administration and trade to financial and real estate operations, company and personal services, education, health and social work. (French Institute of Statistics and Economic Studies, France).

---

is the increase in the proportion of services in economic activity. For France, for example, the proportion of services (mercantile and non-mercantile) was estimated at 25% of the Gross Domestic Product in 1835, rising to 48% in 1959, and now is over 70%, as is the case in the United States.

For Quinn[1], all economic production tends to become a service-based activity, since not only do services account for over two thirds of national production, but also even within commercial concerns the manufacturing operation as such is all too often only a minimal part of the added value as a whole. The rest revolves around the service operations, including research and development, logistics, marketing and finance to purchasing, sales, distribution and after-sales service. Over the past few years, the shift toward the tertiary sector is becoming increasingly common for all productive operations.

This phenomenon becomes even more evident when breaking down the prices of agricultural and industrial products to determine the proportions of their components. A quarter of the price of butter, for example, arises from agricultural work itself, whereas the remaining three quarters correspond to operations of a tertiary nature, for example research, stock management, advertising, distribution, storage and financial services. This process is even more in evidence in the industrial sector. As part of the final value of the products, manufacturing itself accounts for a smaller and smaller proportion, and the processing operations are increasingly shared among a large number of external service providers. For a television set, for example, the percentage of production costs in the retail price is barely 19%, for a car 25%, and for pasta 16%.

---

1. J.B. Quinn, *Intelligent Enterprise*, The Free Press, New York, 1992.

The Case of Alcatel

"Technological developments are constantly reducing the physical content of our added value. The importance of traditional electronics is becoming very minimal. Today, with hindsight, all we can do is reassert our justification for outsourcing many of our production facilities, which can then diversify. All those involved in our sector have unfailingly done what Alcatel has done." Serge Tchuruk, Chairman of Alcatel, in a statement to the newspaper *La Tribune*, January 6, 2004.

All service-based activities can be carried out within production units or be outsourced. However, with the exception of the services making up the core business that companies must keep in their own interest in order to stay alive and in a leading position, as seen above, the other services can be, and more and more frequently are, provided by external specialists.

Thus, employment in industry has been regressing in all major countries. In France, for example, the proportion in employment as a whole fell from 24% in 1980 to 16% in 2002. However, over the past 10 years or so, the added value of the manufacturing industries has been increasing at a higher rate than the economy as a whole, and their productivity has been considerably gaining pace. These results, along with the significant growth in service-sector job creation, can be explained by the strategies of the many companies that focus on their core business and transfer to outside agencies the services or functions that used to be provided within the company structure. Industrial employment is gradually becoming service-oriented employment. One example of this is the Michelin group, the IT services of which are provided by a specialized external company.

The nature of a company's activities is a major aspect that distinguishes one business from another. Most classifications in this field are based on a breakdown to varying degrees of accuracy of the gross domestic product (GDP). The classic division was proposed by Colin Clark[1], who splits national production into three main sectors.

The *primary* sector encompasses activities connected with agriculture, fishing and the extraction of natural resources. The *secondary* sector is concerned with industry in its broadest sense, meaning the transformation of basic products into finished products. The *tertiary* sector groups other activities, essentially services.

---

1. Colin Clark (1905-1989), *Conditions of Economic Progress*, Macmillan, 1940.

This process of division has proved useful for the long-term study of the growth of national economies. The transformation of economic activities implies resorting to such broad categories in order to make comparisons over time.

The disadvantage of such categorization is that within a single sector, completely disparate activities are grouped together. Some authors have even suggested including a quaternary sector covering services based on advanced technologies and with high added value.

Beyond the rationalization of production encouraging the outsourcing of services, changes in demand also incite companies to link an increasingly large proportion of their services to the supply of their industrial products. Such changes make the boundary between industry and services even more artificial, and thus the two sectors are now overlapping in ways never seen before. Industry is becoming "tertiarized" and the tertiary sector is becoming "industrialized".

For Quinn, the key to the success of contemporary companies lies in closer links and alliances with the best firms, wherever in the world they may be based, and whatever area they operate in, from product development and distribution chains to engineering or logistics firms and suppliers of components or subassemblies.

Far more than a mere subcontracting policy, this trend is the manifestation of the "reinvention" of the company seeking to be the best in its field, by concentrating its resources and talents on a few key processes in the value chain, and by setting up a network of partners that are also the best in their field by virtue of their specialization. Symmetrically, when a company has outstanding skills in an internal activity, it can also contemplate making it into a profitable marketable activity and diversify starting from service skills. Today, it is obvious that companies can no longer base their success on their own excellence alone. They must inevitably rely on others, and outsourcing is becoming a necessity. This transformation of production systems falls into the process of which a major part has come to be known as "Laborgistics®".

Defining Laborgistics®[1]

Laborgistisc® is obviously a neologism, a newly coined word. It is a contraction of the Latin term *labor*, meaning "work", and the Greek

----

1. The word "Laborgistics®" was coined and registered by the company International Outsourcing Services (IOS), based in Bloomington, Indiana, USA.

logistikos, which may be translated as "logical thought". In other words, Laborgistics® is a service-oriented activity based on work prepared, organized and executed logically. Laborgistics® is the ability to employ people and technology in unique combinations to address a wide range of solutions. It is strategically oriented and includes multiple firms, partnerships, and critical communication systems.

Laborgistics® forms part of the school of thought known as "concurrent engineering", which consists of involving all the participants in the future production process from the very conception of a product. This implies a joint process favoring the convergence of a number of participants toward a single goal. As Brilman points out[1], in such a process, the sociological principle of participant involvement from the inception of a project replaces the logical yet mechanical principle of sequential action. This leads to global rather than linear management, making it possible from the conception or execution of a project to take into account the constraints and opportunities proposed by those running the production operations.

Concurrent engineering is, in fact, a permanent dialog comparable to an attacking line of rugby players rather than a relay race, as is the case in traditional project management. In fact, it is grounded in the solid organization of team-based work, presenting a transverse vision of development and deploying methods of launching products on the market as quickly as possible. To do so, it shortens the concept stage, during which the choices made determine 80% of later production costs, and tends toward total quality management (TQM) and the "just-in-time" or "tight flow" system. This process, favoring speed, flexibility, coordination and quality, is the frame of reference for Laborgistics®.

The fields to which Laborgistics® can be applied are many and varied, for rather than being an activity based on a precise production function[2], it is a tailor-made activity carried out on behalf of another company. Therefore any sectors of activity may theoretically be concerned by Laborgistics®, as demonstrated by the following examples.

---

1. *Op. cit.*

2. A production function is a precise technological relation between the quantity of goods produced and the quantity of production factors used in the process. It expresses the production process, i.e. the choice of the combination of factors decided upon.

Multi-Sector Laborgistics®

International Outsourcing Services (IOS) is a Franco-American company specializing in Laborgistics® and active in extremely varied sectors, as shown below.

– IOS organizes the assembly of armchairs and sofas in Juarez in Mexico, for the Brown Jordan company, as part of a contract signed for several years with the Marriott and Holiday Inn hotel chains. This agreement provides for the production of 1.5 million items a year.

– IOS completes the assembly of cellular phone cigarette lighter chargers for use in cars, manufactured by the International Components Corporation (ICC) in China, and ships them to RadioShack distribution centers all over the United States. This contract is worth 1.5 million dollars a year.

– IOS has developed an automated system for checking credit card signatures in order to avoid disputes. It operates this checking system for the Raph divisions of the Kroger company, and the latter was able to make a saving of 1.2 million dollars in three months.

– IOS packages and distributes the entire production of a multi-purpose recycled glass abrasive for Earthstone International. In this example, IOS carries out almost all the operations, from supplies, engineering and packaging to manufacture, distribution and after-sales service. The only aspects it is not directly involved in are research and development, marketing and general management.

These examples show that IOS goes far beyond mere subcontracting or classic outsourcing. It applies the principles of Laborgistics® in the form of near partnerships in quite different sectors.

Laborgistics® often resembles what is referred to as "contract manufacturing", which consists in deciding that for certain companies production is no longer part of their core business, and that they should entrust it to other companies that have become specialized in it.

A company using this method of production may then concentrate on research and development, marketing and distribution, while other outside partners become specialized in certain components. Naturally, the objective is to increase flexibility when faced with variations in demand, which is becoming increasingly unpredictable as a result of the globalization of economies. However, outsourcing in the form of "contract manufacturing" does not only consist of determining which services should be carried out or which products should be manufactured externally, it also requires that control methods and means be set out in contractual terms. This makes it possible to deal with any departures from the projected norms when necessary. In short, this new form of production requires new managerial skills.

Thus, between 2001 and 2003, the Alcatel group, one of the largest telecommunications parts manufacturers in the world, parted with 49 of the 100 sites it owned, leading to the departure of over 18,000 staff. As S. Tchuruk, its CEO, put it, "Alcatel will soon be a company with no factories". The objective of the company is not only to reduce costs in the short term, but also to gain flexibility and above all to turn fixed costs into variable costs, since predictable activity levels never remain constant. At Alcatel, it is considered that in general it takes two years to balance out costs between internal and external production. Additionaly by concentrating on its core business, Alcatel started to take on a symmetrical structure, for at the same time, it specialized in network maintenance contracts for several telecommunications operators that in turn chose to outsource this function. The French firm has recently taken on over 600 staff for this new activity.

Laborgistics® is part of a long-term view of company strategies. By making production constraints more flexible, it makes it possible to innovate and improve performance. It is thus not a question of seeking competitiveness at any price by merely reducing labor costs, thereby entailing the kind of anemia that can be found in some companies that have become listless. It is by no means a model based on the systematic effort to reduce staffing levels.

However, being successful means finding and implementing new skills based on legal and technical know-how and solid managerial abilities. The specialists in the purchasing function, who have historically managed traditional subcontracting and outsourcing operations, are no longer sufficient to run this new type of activity.

Laborgistics® is part of the development of outsourcing, which has changed dramatically over the last 30 years. According to Miliotis and Mayeur[1], there are three generations of coexisting outsourcing methods:

– *Conventional* outsourcing, the oldest form, the objective of which is essentially to reduce costs, and that came into being in the

---

1. P. Miliotis is chairman of the French Outsourcing Commission and C. Mayeur is the director of Skills Action Sensation.

1980s. This concerns simple operational tasks (catering, cleaning, etc.) that are entrusted to specialists.

– *Collaborative* outsourcing originated in the 1990s, and while still aiming at reducing costs it is also intended to generate greater flexibility. This gave rise, for example, to facilities management and the drafting of contracts resembling partnerships with outside service providers.

– *Transformative* outsourcing is presented by the authors as being the third age of outsourcing, when a company focuses on a kind of knowledge-based economics centered on alliance, interdependence and shared responsibility. In other words, it is the essence of Laborgistics®, the most highly evolved form of outsourcing.

Over the past several years, there has been a shift from simple cost reduction and flexibility to improved results through the transformation of both production processes and the organizations themselves.

The advent of Laborgistics®, as a response to the real needs of companies facing ever harsher competition, was also triggered by two factors that have transformed production conditions and human activity: first, the technical progress arising from the new information and communication technologies; second, legal and institutional changes brought about by the deregulation process.

The Role of Information Technology Companies

Time and space constraints have now disappeared thanks to the technical progress made not only in information technology but also, and above all, in telecommunications, notably through the construction of fixed or mobile broadband networks able to transmit speech, data, text and fixed or animated images, and through the development of services operating on fixed or mobile networks such as the Internet. Long-distance communication, i.e. telecommunications, is now transforming the way we exchange information on the basis of three main characteristics: mobility, interoperability[1] and interactivity.

The new opportunities offered by technology lead to significant changes in production methods. A growing quantity of information is integrated into the equipment, the efficient use of which requires

---

1. Interoperability means that all networks and terminals can be compatible for communication purposes.

Telecommunications Expenditure

A survey of French companies employing more than 10,000 staff carried out in 2001 by the Audoin consultancy firm for the telecommunications regulation authority (ART), shows that in 1999, the companies allotted the following funds:

– 1.3% of their annual turnover for telecommunications, i.e. EUR 2,400 euros per employee[a] and twice that figure, almost EUR 4,800 for IT, including both services and equipment;

– each employee thus requires an average of EUR 7,200 a year for information and communication technologies.

a. These figures vary according to the sector, ranging from 0.39% of turnover for trade (some EUR 800) to 5.2% for banking (some EUR 8,000).

---

increasing recourse to intangible capital. To a certain extent, the phenomenon is paradoxical, in that research and development make it possible to build up a capital of knowledge leading to the emergence of ever more powerful equipment, but the use of this equipment requires an extra input of intangible capital.

This transformation is not limited to productive activities; it concerns the overall functioning of firms and thereby has a major impact on all the management practices within companies.

The introduction of information-based technologies into the process of exchange between suppliers and customers makes it possible to improve its efficiency by reducing costs and increasing speed. However, it also results in an alteration of the nature of the relations among those playing the economic game and in a change in the conditions of competition. This phenomenon concerns both relations among firms as well as between companies and the final users of the products and services.

The primacy of the principal over the external service provider is tending, in practice, to weaken because of the need for active cooperation among companies. However, this has led to the emergence of new problems. For example, who has the right of ownership over a product developed jointly by a company's research department and its suppliers? The question is more generally one of sharing the profits of a creative activity developed as a joint project. In such cases it is always difficult to determine the contribution, and therefore the rights, of each of those involved.

The boom in the new information and communication technologies over the last 15 years has provided new opportunities for implementing and managing production processes differently. These technologies are at the source of three types of innovation:

– First, they now make possible what was previously impossible. This is known as *product* or *service* innovation. This was the case, for example, of the emergence of common use of microchip-bearing credit cards to identify the holder and simplify transactions.

– Second, they provide the means to enhance existing production methods, meaning the improved performance of tasks that were already performed. This is known as *process* innovation, one example is the automation of certain tasks.

– Finally, *organization* innovation provides the opportunity to modify organization in order to do what was done before, but differently. They lead to a change in the very concept of the production system and the relationship among its components, i.e. the value chain.

In short, the new technologies provide a means to work differently.

The Impact of the Opening of Markets and Borders

The institutional framework in which companies operate also plays a particularly important part in their development and in economic growth in general. When institutional structures are ill suited or inefficient, growth is not stimulated and may even regress. For Douglass North (Nobel Prize laureate 1993), Western Europe and the United States have been, in the past, wise enough to set up political systems that made such growth possible[1].

This is what has been happening once again since the late 1970s in the wake of the deregulation trend. In their groundbreaking work, economists such as Stigler[2] (Nobel Prize laureate 1982) have insisted since the Second World War on a philosophical conception of society, leading them to adopt the principle that any economic system must first and foremost favor the consumer, and that the consumer enjoys a greater number of advantages when production costs are at their lowest. For Stigler, the only system that brings about such a result is the market economy with a maximum level of competition.

---

1. D. North, *Institutions, Institutional Change and Economic Performance*, Cambridge University Press, 1990.

2. G. Stigler, *Citizen and the State: Essays on Regulation*, Chicago University Press, 1975.

These ideas were back on the agenda following the serious economic problems encountered by the United States in the late 1970s, particularly a sharp rise in inflation and a drop in productivity. According to most economists, these difficulties stemmed, among other factors, from an excess of bureaucracy, the shortsightedness of company managers and the noncommittal role of the state. The watchword of the time, which was to become very popular, was to demand that public authorities ceased to intervene in economic activity. The underlying economic hypothesis was that companies were more efficient if the state stayed as far away as possible from the business world, since public authority intervention invariably gave rise to perverse effects that were far more harmful than the original problem. Stigler has shown, for example, that in the early 1980s, the federal government had allotted a subsidy to apiarists whose bees were dying because of pollution. He goes on to say that the consumer gained nothing, but that once the measure was implemented no more bees were dying natural deaths in North America!

Deregulation consists in encouraging the market as far as is possible and spurning the private or public monopolies that had been designed on the basis of the theory of the natural monopoly, notably in such fields as telecommunications, air transportation and energy. This means questioning the concept of the welfare state, which for Stigler is no more than "a shortsighted Robin Hood who steals from everyone and gives to many – and not only to the poor – the fraction of the spoils that is left over after the deduction of significant administration costs".

This institutional change has naturally led to changes in management practices. A notable aspect of this is the decentralization of the decision-making process, more particularly the wish to sound out the market, meaning to seek out skills, new partnerships and specialists from outside. In a word, people have been looking for high-performance partners.

By changing the institutional rules, deregulation has brought about a change in the framework within which production and exchange activities take place. It has created factors favorable to the development of Laborgistics®. As seen above, it should not be forgotten that at the same time there was a movement encouraging the abolition of customs barriers and the implementation of conditions favoring free exchange. This new conception of international relations, the smooth running of which is handled by the World Trade Organization, has made it possible not only to determine new openings but also to set up areas favorable to all specialized activities involving outsourcing and thus Laborgistics®.

For Krugman[1], the promotion and organization of a relatively free world in terms of trade is among the major steps forward at the end of the 20th century. Almost everyone today considers that the development of international exchange is a good thing. Deregulation ultimately consists in removing as many obstacles to liberty as possible, in order to be committed to seeking the most active interplay between the laws of supply and demand.

It should also be noted that "the two Ms" – marketing and multimedia (telecommunications, IT and television) – complement one another, since by linking people up, independently of their geographic location, multimedia activities have led to the emergence of a truly global market conducive to new forms of organization and production such as Laborgistics®.

Laborgistics® in Practice

Laborgistics® can only be incorporated into an anticipatory view of the nature of the company. It is applied to a variety of situations with the general objective of seeking the maximum long-term competitive advantage. This objective can only be reached by seeking innovative capacities outside the company. Far from consisting merely of purchasing means, Laborgistics® implies seeking results, leading naturally to true partnerships among firms expressed in terms of reciprocal commitment.

Trans-Frontier Laborgistics®

In 2003, a French service company having recourse to hi-tech operations chose to build a plant in Slovakia. While there were economic reasons for this choice, there was far more to it. It is true that in Slovakia the average gross monthly wage is low (EUR 300) and the unemployment rate is high. Traditionally, labor is of high quality and the current stable political and financial situation encourages the arrival of foreign investment.

Slovakia is soon to become a full member of the European Union, which will guarantee that the company's partners and clients can be sure of operating with the same standards and regulations as in France.

---

1. P. Krugman, *The Age of Diminished Expectations: U.S. Policy in the 1990s*, MIT Press, 1997.

International Outsourcing Services (IOS) is a Franco-American company set up in France following the acquisition of family companies specialized in data inputting and promotional campaign management. It digitizes and indexes paper documents and electronic images for various sectors, including distribution, banking, transport and pension plans. It is a sector calling on both labor and, increasingly, high technology.

Operators are indispensable for inputting and for controlling the most powerful computers and the most sophisticated scanners. The financial, commercial and insurance documents processed demand much rigor and considerable professional diligence.

The unit set up in Bratislava combines technology and human capacities. The operators receive on screen documents such as checks and complaint slips scanned in France, often in real time, or electronic images. The information is then forwarded through secured broadband networks.

The Slovak operators read the images, validate them or add to them if necessary, then format them in electronic files. The completed and verified databases are subsequently sent back to France in order to update marketing files or client accounts.

This unit was set up abroad in order to meet the demands of certain clients in terms of speed, by being able to work when the French sites are closed. For example, check deposit slips can be prepared and simple information can be processed at lower cost.

Slovakia was chosen over China because the linguistic and cultural barriers were easier to overcome, and because the regulations in terms of transport, insurance and labor law are soon to be the same as in France. In addition, Bratislava is only three hours away from France by air and road, which makes it easier to supervise on-site operations.

IOS has thus transferred its know-how, and the operators formerly in the Champagne region have become supervisors in Slovakia, passing on their skills. The ISO 9001 certification procedure implemented simultaneously on several sites has also led the teams to reconsider, transpose and validate their own procedures. Finally, it should be added that IOS has transferred considerable assets – several million euros – to equip the site with the latest technology.

This example shows Laborgistics® at work, as the ultimate form of outsourcing. For IOS, setting up part of its processing chain in Slovakia means that its clients benefit from shorter reaction times, and that the company is able to offer new services by using information that previously could not be managed in France.

The Specific Characteristics of Laborgistics®

Laborgistics® is distinct in various ways from previous models in terms of having recourse to the market. It may be considered that there are four options for a company seeking the outside resources it feels it needs in order to reach its production objectives: the straightforward purchase of production factors, subcontracting, outsourcing and Laborgistics®.

As the above table shows, the various types of recourse to the market bear on different aspects, operate under specific conditions

Comparative Table of Types of Recourse to the Market

	Purchasing	**Subcontracting**	**Outsourcing**	**Laborgistics®**
Needs	Input (or production factor)	Variation in production, saving on costs	Savings on costs, searching for new competencies	New production organization
Type of product	Goods and services	Goods and services	Goods and services	Services only
Time scale	Short- or very short-term	Short-term	Medium-term	Medium- and long-term
Type of relationship	Buyer/seller	Partner	Strategic partner	Alliances
Nature of recourse to market	Precise and well defined	Well defined and based on the expertise of the service provider	Progressive and grounded in the expertise of the service provider	Constantly evolving
Management	Operational	Tactical	Strategic	Strategic
Role of information technologies	Minimal	Minimal	Significant	Essential
Keys to success (*)	Quality and openness	Performance and reliability	Efficiency and new organizational structure	Rapid response and flexibility
Expected gain	Low-cost production factors	Savings on costs	Savings on costs and flexibility	Rapid response and flexibility revenue enhancement
Organization	Purchasing department	Purchasing department	Purchasing department but decision by general management	Specialized service under the supervision of the general manager

(*) The characteristics of the keys to success are cumulative from one type of recourse to another.

according to the choices made and lead to different functioning methods and objectives.

– The purchase of production factors (inputs) required for reaching the company's objectives, i.e. useful for its production function, concerns goods and services and is carried out over a short time scale. Such purchases are repeated at regular intervals in order to respond to production needs. The ensuing relationships with suppliers can be encountered in any exchange between buyer and seller, with the former wishing to obtain the lowest price possible and to set competing suppliers against one another, and the latter hoping to sell their products at the highest price possible while at the same time fostering customer loyalty. Generally, purchasing is related to goods and services specifically defined by the specialized department within the company, usually the purchasing department. This technical function comes under the heading of operational management, and its key factors to success imply the products purchased being of the highest possible quality and available at the right time – if possible following the "just-in-time" principle – in order to avoid any interruption in the activities of the company.

– The main objective of subcontracting is to enable a company to respond to fluctuations in its activities as economically as possible. Naturally, such operations have a bearing on goods and services of very different types, but are nonetheless purely tactical, all the more since they are generally carried out over a relatively short period of time. Subcontracting comes under the responsibility of the purchasing department, which must determine the number and quantities of items to be produced externally. While maintaining close relationships with the suppliers, this department must constantly play competitors against one another. For this type of activity, the impact of information and communication technologies remains minimal[1]. However, the key factor to success lies in the performance and reliability of the subcontractors, wherever in the world they may be. While the outside service provider enjoys a certain autonomy in accomplishing its tasks, its links with the principal vary according to the importance of the activity with which it is entrusted. The contract may equally concern the manufacture of a part or component or the assembly of a subsystem such as an air-

---

1. Business-to-Business (B2B) operations carried out over the Internet are becoming more widespread.

plane engine. It is obvious that the relationships are different in these two cases.

– Outsourcing implies a close relationship between the company and its outside service provider. An important activity can only be outsourced as part of a medium- to long-term arrangement, thus forming part of a strategic partnership. When deciding on this type of activity, it is invariably a question of seeking to save on costs, but outsourcing goes far beyond this, in that its main objective is to acquire competencies from a genuine specialist. This is clearly a strategic decision on the part of the management, although it is most often the purchasing department that implements and monitors operations. Information and communication technologies play a major role in outsourcing, as their contribution, to both product design and management methods is particularly useful. Lastly, outsourcing naturally leads to changes in the organization of production, thereby ensuring greater efficiency and above all greater flexibility in order to rise to the medium-term challenges of a hypercompetitive environment.

– Finally, Laborgistics® is the most highly developed method of having recourse to the market. It forms part of the conceptual framework of network companies, which are flexible, adaptive structures mobilizing – and no longer possessing – a coordinated, stable set of competencies. It is a response to the quest for a new form of produc-

---

The Case of IBM

In the early 1990s, the computer giant IBM, with its 400,000 workers and losses of $8 billion in 1993, found itself in a critical situation.

It was at that time that Lou Gerstner was appointed president, and decided to tackle the problem head-on. He laid off thousands of workers, closed half the factories and outsourced many activities by selling, for example, the hard disk production units and subcontracting the assembly of the computers. He concentrated on core competencies, dramatically increased the number of partnerships, in short, he turned "Big Blue" into a provider of integrated solutions.

Lou Gerstner, as he states in his most recent book[a], concentrates the entire company on service activities, which in 2003 accounted for almost 50% of its turnover.

With its e-business model, IBM has thus now become a service-based company, responding to the outsourcing needs of its clients.

a. *Who Says Elephants Can't Dance?*, HarperBusiness, 2002.

tion organization, using all the opportunities offered by information and communication technologies. This type of strategic decision is made with a time scale of at least five years in mind, and is based on relationships among partners that can almost be qualified as alliances. To ensure its smooth running and monitoring, Laborgistics® requires the support of a specialized service made up of managers able to integrate all the composite parts of the value chain of the company. The success of this mode of organization depends on its preparation and its technical, economic and social integration into the company that sets it up. The ultimate aim is to attain the most rapid response possible when faced with market developments. However, it should not be forgotten that Laborgistics® leads to a reexamination of the organization and functioning of the company as a whole when setting up this type of activity.

Is a Laborgistics®-Oriented Company Just One of the Crowd?

Companies wishing to put Laborgistics® into practice follow exactly the same strategic method as other companies, according to their objectives, their age and their size.

The first choice companies have to make is to decide whether they should concentrate their efforts on a single activity or to spread them out among many. However, in between specializing and setting up a multitude of production units, there are many intermediate situations, such as alliances and cooperation programs between companies. These same questions arise in firms that have chosen to implement Laborgistics® for other companies.

Generally speaking, these are recently established or small firms that are compelled to adopt a specialization strategy. The reason for this is the low level of resources available; it has proved more efficient to concentrate them on a single product in order to take the greatest advantage of potential economies of scale.

Larger companies very rarely manufacture a single product. However, some of them do limit their activities to products closely related with one another.

This policy, known as differentiation, is a less developed, though no less real, form of specialization, with all the advantages and disadvantages it entails.

Limited diversity of activities allows for a greater concentration of the firm's resources, in terms of both logistics and management. It is thus possible, thanks to economies of scale, to reduce the average costs. Similarly, the strategic objectives are not so varied. It is thus easier to define them and determine what means must be deployed to reach them. Finally, information needs are reduced, which implies more accurate knowledge of the company's immediate environment.

In certain cases, specialization[1] may go hand-in-hand with a standardization of the supply, since the physical characteristics of the products within a given differentiated group are rigorously identical. This is the policy implemented by certain hotel and fast food chains (McDonald's and its Big Mac, for example). This presents a twofold advantage. First, it makes it possible to define standard production procedures, for which the costs of design and development can be offset by large-scale production, thus leading to economies of scale. It therefore makes economic sense to carry out in-depth, and therefore costly, research in order to define the procedures enabling the firm to obtain a product of stable quality at a lower cost. Second, this standardization reduces the costs of information research by the customer base, according to Ackerlof (Nobel Prize laureate 2001)[2]. A burger at Burger King, for example, is produced using the same procedure and the same ingredients in New York, Sydney and London. It is not necessarily the best burger available in these cities, but the customer is fully aware of its characteristics even before buying it.

The limits of a specialization policy are the other side of the coin. The first limit is the vulnerability of the company. An unfavorable economic context in the sector, the arrival of substitute products or new competition can have severely negative effects on its situation, and even cast doubts over its future by reducing its only source of revenue. Furthermore, the specialization of the workforce, the resources and the internal organization methods that result from it may lead to an overly rigid structure making it difficult, if not impossible, to adapt as necessary when entering the maturity phase in the product's life cycle. More particularly, the information systems are not designed to monitor the environment and detect opportunities for change. One final limit is the narrowness of development prospects, as the field of possible activities is itself reduced. The specialization strategy leads companies to emphasize profita-

---

1. Laborgistics®-based firms are highly specialized, in the field of information and data processing, for example.

2. G. Ackerlof, "The Market for Lemons: Quality Uncertainty and the Market Mechanism", in *Quarterly Journal of Economics*, August 1970.

bility rather than growth. This is the reason why it can never be adopted by large-scale companies.

Companies offering specialized Laborgistics®-based activities are generally small or young companies, but as they grow they are forced to broaden the range of their activities. The corollary of a company's growth is the necessary diversification of its activities, and their product range thus becomes wider. This expansion can occur using various methods that are not incompatible with one another. Their common feature, however, is that they use a lot of resources.

A product is generally defined on the basis of the three principal aspects of company policy. The first is *strategic* marketing: what is the need or function we wish to satisfy and how are we to do so? The second is the *sales* policy, which consists in defining, and if necessary segmenting, the target customer base. Finally, the third aspect is connected with the *technological* choices influencing the production process that has been set up. In other words, a product may be defined by three characteristics: need, market and technology.

Diversification is a policy of multiple production in which the products differ from one another in at least two of their characteristics. Two main categories of diversification can thus be distinguished: proximity diversification and lateral diversification. In the first case, only two characteristics are modified, whereas in the second, the three characteristics change.

In the case of proximity diversification, the characteristic that remains stable is the element common to the various activities of the company, and thus constitutes its avenue for development. The firm makes the most of its intangible assets of knowledge, know-how and information sharing for a variety of products, thus taking advantage of economies of scale. It could be the mastery of a given technique (for example BIC and the manufacture of molded plastic products), the intimate knowledge of a market and the advantageous use of a brand image (for example LVMH and the luxury goods market) or the ability to satisfy a need (for example pharmaceutical laboratories).

In its implementation methods, diversification may be internal or external. If it opts for the internal method, the firm lays the foundations of a new activity. However, if it opts for the external method, i.e. the acquisition of patents, licenses or entire companies, these bases already exist and more often than not function well. The most frequent form is diversification through absorption.

The external method, when this is possible[1], is often preferred. The main reason for this preference is connected with the risk implicit in any diversification policy. It is a crucial decision, and given the scale of the resources it mobilizes and the ensuing effects on the established activities, it may call into question the very survival of the company. It is therefore vital to limit risks as much as possible. Diversification requires not only real investments in terms of production and sales, but also the investment of intangible capital in terms of new competencies relating to the two characteristics that have been modified. It is thus tempting to acquire means that are already operational and for which the value of this intangible capital may be estimated on the basis of past performance rather than commitment to expenditure that is generally underestimated with a view to setting up a unit with as yet unknown profitability. A further advantage of this policy is that it makes it possible to gain immediate access to an already existing sector of the market. This results in progress in terms of the development of turnover and, depending on the case, fewer random elements inherent in the accession to a new market.

The concern with limiting risks also explains why proximity diversification is often preferred, and why lateral diversification is only seen as the extension of this first step. In proximity diversification, there are fewer new skills to be acquired, and therefore the risk is not so great.

The main advantages of successful diversification lie in the opportunities for growth that it offers and in the decreased vulnerability of the company with regard to competition and to the economic fluctuations on each of the markets where the company operates. This is what explains the attraction of such a policy. Thus, many Laborgistics®-based companies that were initially highly specialized later start on the road to diversification.

Furthermore, it can be noted that markets are going global and that companies must increasingly integrate the international dimension into their strategies. In this respect, two major options are open to them. The first consists in exporting, and the second in setting up abroad. The second solution is only justified when the volume of business abroad is sufficient. However, more and more firms are doing so, particularly those adopting a Laborgistics®-based approach.

----

1. There must naturally be firms already undertaking the activities required, which is not the case when the product is all-new.

At the moment, two main reasons for going multinational can be distinguished: the wish or obligation to come into closer contact with the foreign markets where the production is sold, and the search for advantages in terms of costs[1]. It may be added that when a national market is small, internationalization is the only way that the companies can grow.

Historical, cultural and economic differences explain why consumer preferences vary from one country to another. Companies wishing to set up on a number of national markets must take into account the diversity in tastes and behavior patterns when they develop their offer. Their production and sales policies must be appropriate to multiple situations. As soon as the volume of business makes it possible to do so, it is therefore preferable to relocate production itself, in order to locate it in proximity to the markets it is aiming at. As information is circulating more quickly and the transportation of products is easier, it is now possible to detect and remedy any quantitative and qualitative disparities that may appear between supply and demand. Other aspects that may influence the general choice of geographical location, such as how perishable the goods are or how heavy to transport they may be, must also be taken into account.

The second major reason for going multinational is the desire to reduce costs. Companies set up in countries where certain production factors, most frequently the labor force, cost less than elsewhere. The production coming from such a system is primarily targeted at the richer countries, where the demand is greatest. Southeast Asia and the free zones located in Mexico along the United States border[2], are the favored localities for such subsidiaries.

One final aspect of the globalization of activities in general is the phenomenon of globalization of certain markets. According to Porter[3],

---

1. The explanation linked with the differences in localization between seams of natural resources and transformation operations is no longer applicable, and furthermore was inaccurate. This form of becoming multinational was grounded in the absence of certain factors necessary for production (financial resources and technical skills) in the countries, often underdeveloped, where the natural resources lay. That natural resource extraction industries could be nationalized shows that localization, which has not changed, was not the fundamental reason for going multinational.

2. The city of Juarez in Mexico, for example, is located on one bank of the Rio Grande, and El Paso, Texas, in on the other.

3. *Op. cit.*

a market is global when the competitive position of a company is significantly affected by its position in other countries, and vice versa. This situation is opposed to that of companies having multiple bases, fragmented worldwide according to the needs of various national markets. Competition among global firms happens on a worldwide homogeneous market, and there are no longer any local niches in which certain companies are protected from their foreign competitors. The formulation of their strategy must take into account their geographical interdependence and use the new opportunity for action that this offers. Boeing, for example, considering itself to be under attack from Airbus on the American market, may retaliate by taking action on the Japanese market.

Not all activities are affected by globalization, which can only arise when it is possible to set up a certain global standardization of the product on the basis of the three characteristics. The first step is to ensure that the needs the company wishes to satisfy and the behavior patterns of the customer base are, or can be made, identical[1]. The technical dimension exerts less direct influence, because, if the first two conditions are fulfilled, the cost constraints imply that the companies commit themselves to closer involvement. For these reasons, sectors such as electronics aimed at the general public or professionals, airlines, motorcycles and drinks may be considered global. However, by the same token, this includes luxury goods and television series[2]. It has now become clear that globalization for Laborgistics®-based activities is beginning to develop, as shown, for example, by the case of IBM, which has chosen to refocus on e-business.

Between the absolute segmentation by national markets and total globalization, there are many intermediate situations. It is for the companies to identify them, perhaps to modify them, and to formulate their strategies accordingly.

The various internationalization strategies mentioned above can only be implemented if companies build up structures appropriate to their choices. The organizational methods can vary according to

---

1. Marketing policy can play a major role in this field, by either eliminating or reinforcing specific national characteristics.

2. The current international failure of French production in terms of television is not due, as is often claimed, to linguistic difficulties, but to the refusal to acknowledge the global nature of the market. The success of German series is the exception that proves the rule.

the circumstances. But whatever the situation, it is important to bring together management flexibility, economy of scale, synergy, and a global vision of the firm's business. Decentralized organization, by geographical area or product line, according to the degree of globalization of the markets, combined with a clear separation of operational and strategic responsibilities, makes it possible to reconcile – at least in part – these opposing imperatives.

Conditions for Success and Precautions to be Taken

The success of Laborgistics®, given its strategic nature, requires taking a certain number of precautions. Most notably, the contract between a company and its external service provider plays a pivotal role, far more important than a simple subcontracting agreement or the outsourcing of primary functions as in catering or janitor services. In this type of activity, in the event of a disagreement, all the partners have to do is part company, and the party requiring the service simply goes to look for suppliers on the market. The suppliers are all the more replaceable since subcontracting activities tend to occur in the short term.

On the other hand, when recourse to external agencies concerns major activities, and when Laborgistics® becomes an essential element in the functioning of the company, the contract binding the two parties, its execution and its monitoring are of paramount importance.

Laborgistics® is not limited to a mere contractual relationship. It leads to the reconsideration of the various structures of the company, and the collaboration between the service providers and the company can no longer be seen in terms of a power struggle but in terms of shared responsibility. Nonetheless, everything starts with a real contract built up through the negotiation process that happens in several stages.

The contract stage of a Laborgistics®-based undertaking is a decision that should never be rushed. It is generally considered that the preparation for such a process takes at least nine months of reflection, and that most failures in this field arise from a slipshod contract that has not taken the whole problem into account.

The first stage consists in identifying the functions to which Laborgistics® could or should be applied and those that the company wishes to retain as part of its core business. At this stage, it should not be forgotten that the matter must be broached with all the staff in order to curb any cultural reticence that may hinder the process.

The second stage – just as important as the first – is the selection of the service provider, which must clearly offer a quality of service at least as high as that offered internally. It must also be able to adapt to the specific characteristics of the company in order to be able to work in partnership. This is why it is indispensable to select several companies before making the final choice.

The third essential stage consists in choosing the external service provider with which to actually collaborate. Various criteria come into play here, including the following:

– The quality of the service. For obvious reasons, it is wiser to prefer the service providers having started a certification procedure such as obtaining ISO 9000.

– The capacity to respect deadlines and work in a tight-flow system.

– The capacity for innovation, in order to be sure of benefiting from the finest production processes.

– The durability of the service provider, in order to be sure it will complete its undertakings by exploiting its customer portfolio, or the state of its finances, particularly its cash flow.

– Its commitment and its respect of the specifications.

All contracts must be as precise as possible in order to protect the company using Laborgistics®. As it means a long-term commitment, a certain interdependence is formed between the principal and the external service provider. Consequently, the contract becomes an essential vector for monitoring and protection.

The purpose of the fourth stage is to draw up the specifications, taking into account many factors, including the following:

– the trial period;

– the scope of the operation;

– the confidentiality of the data provided;

– the expected performance and the indicators selected to measure it;

– accepted deadlines;

– penalties;

– shared responsibilities;

– guarantee of continuity;

– conditions of termination or cancellation.

All specifications must be precise and detailed, and be drawn up after negotiation between the two parties. This may take several months, and will not be definitive before the end of the trial period.

Finally, it must be understood that Laborgistics® is not merely a management method, but a fundamental trend leading to the reorganization of the scope of corporate business. It is thus necessary to take into account the impact it may have on the employees in terms of cohesion and sense of belonging to the company, and to take a certain number of precautions before setting out.

Once the Laborgistics® process is underway, there must naturally be a monitoring mechanism in the form of a specially designed unit bringing together the people qualified to ensure this.

Given the strategic nature of Laborgistics®, members of different departments – technical, financial, purchasing, legal and human resources – must be brought together, with the participation of the CEO. Regular reporting should be planned to keep all those involved in the project informed of developments.

Beyond the financial advantages and flexibility it offers, well-designed Laborgistics® makes it possible to forge a partnership between the principal company and its external service provider. To do so, those involved have to agree to change their behavior, learning to share rather than protect themselves, which ultimately leads to changes in organizational structures. Setting up a partnership means redefining the roles and powers of each major function involved in the relationship. With the development of Laborgistics® there is a tendency to adopt project-oriented structures. The functional divisions are complemented by a transverse organization that increasingly encourages working in teams.

Measuring Performance

To study the performance of Laborgistics®, the SWOT model can be used: Strengths, Weaknesses, Opportunities and Threats. This is a commonly used diagnostic tool, with which, for a given project, it is possible to analyze the external environment (opportunities and threats) and the internal environment (strengths and weaknesses).

In the analysis of the external environment, the opportunities form the field of action in which the project may hope to obtain a differential edge over its competitors. Thus, a company will be in this situation when thanks to Laborgistics®, its own competencies enable it to make the most of an opportunity more easily than its competitors, i.e. to make the most of its key factors for success. Threats are problems caused by an unfavorable trend or a disturbance in the environment hampering the execution of the project.

Measuring the Performance of Laborgistics®

Internal Environment

Strengths	Weaknesses
– Increased flexibility	– Absence of capacity to innovate in service provider
– Lower costs	– Lack of experience of service provider
– Refocusing on core business	– Loss of cohesion within the company
– Transformation of fixed costs into variable costs	– Dependence on service provider

External Environment

Opportunities	Threats
– Partnership	– Defective management of service provider
– Access to competencies	– Loss of know-how
– Transformation of the organization	– Social risks
– Better value labor force	– Hidden costs

However, in the internal environment, the strengths and weaknesses are assessed according to criteria linked to their performance and their importance in the strategy of the company.

Thus, the decision-making criteria and measurement of the performance of a Laborgistics®-based operation can be presented in a SWOT matrix, as shown below.

On the basis of these various factors bearing on both the specific nature of Laborgistics® and the aspects that must be taken into account to ensure its successful implementation, it is possible to evoke a certain number of rules to be respected, which might be termed the "ten commandments of Laborgistics®".

The market for Laborgistics® and outsourcing in Europe is now worth about 200 billion dollars. The growth rate for BPO (Business Process Outsourcing), which brings together all the functional aspects of companies, from purchasing and facilities management to accounting and logistics, is expected to grow by almost 12% a year for several years[1]. It is thus clear that this market is expanding

---

1. Source: IDC (International Data Corporation).

The Ten Commandments of Laborgistics®

1- Laborgistics® must always be part of a strategic operation.

2- Laborgistics® is not a solution to management errors.

3- Laborgistics® does not only help reduce costs; it plays a considerable role in product design as well as cost-effectiveness.

4- Laborgistics® requires shared culture in terms of both management and specialization.

5- Laborgistics® can only be applied in the long term, with contracts running over several years.

6- Laborgistics® requires service providers with great human and technical potential.

7- Laborgistics® can be applied to all support services.

8- Laborgistics® does not signify simply paying for means, but paying for results.

9- Laborgistics® has no geographical boundaries, but must respect company law and international codes of ethics.

10- Laborgistics® leads to partnerships, in which "win-win" relationships are fostered.

---

rapidly in all countries and will continue to do so. Laborgistics® is becoming an essential element in all production systems.

CHAPTER 5 :

The Consequences of Laborgistics®

Unlike subcontracting or simple outsourcing, Laborgistics®, through its strategic nature and its increasing importance in companies, has a manifold impact both on management itself and economic activity in general. In other words, Laborgistics® has an impact both microeconomic and macroeconomic.

Microeconomic Influences

The purpose of refocusing on core business, which is a prerequisite for any Laborgistics®-base activity, is to simplify the management of companies by reducing the scale and limiting the diversity of their activities. At the same time, they benefit from the division of labor, which, according to the principles of economic analysis, makes it possible to increase productivity.

For several years now there has been a consensus among specialists in the field, who consider that management is the science and practice of government as applied to organizations and more specifically to companies. However, governing means making decisions in many fields. The multidimensional nature of organizations the complexity of their functioning means that management is subdivided into a number of sub-disciplines. Some of these are specialized and lay the emphasis on a given activity. Others bear on the interdependence of these activities, analyzing the ways in which they complement or oppose one another within the functioning processes.

The operations carried out by companies are divided according to the specialization criteria, and this leads to the fragmenting of the company into major functions. As a rule, six major functions can be discerned:

- management function;
- sales function (marketing);
- production function;
- accounting function and management monitoring (which are more and more frequently dissociated);
- financial function;
- human resources function.

A particular aspect of management is associated with each of these fields of activity. However, it would be far too reductive to regard organizations and simple juxtapositions of largely independent functions, although this may prove useful at the initial stages of analysis. It is reasonable to complement such an approach with more transverse considerations, shedding light on the existence of interactions among these different aspects in the ways in which organizations function. In both planning and action, it is thus necessary to consider questions linked to internal structures, information and communication systems and the development and implementation of overall policy.

As seen in the previous chapters, Laborgistics® is an essential element in management methods for today's companies, and its strategic role has an impact not only on the general functioning of companies but also on the various functions within the company.

Laborgistics® will have a significant effect on **the financial function** within companies. It should be recalled that this function serves three main purposes:

- ensuring permanently the day-to-day financing of the production, i.e. managing cash flow;
- procuring the means of payment necessary for the production in the long term, i.e. financing investments and growth;
- obtaining financial means at the lowest cost to avoid increasing company expenditure.

By having an increasing number of operations carried out by external service providers, companies using Laborgistics® transform costs that were originally fixed into variable costs. By placing orders with an outside service provider, the company using Laborgistics® no longer needs to invest in equipment or facilities to fuel production entrusted to outside suppliers. In addition, at the same time, staffing, which is more and more commonly seen as a fixed cost in view of the constraints imposed by labor law, is also becoming a variable factor, and with Laborgistics® its proportion of total outgoings is diminishing.

Thus, with recourse to the market, the financial means necessary for the functioning of the company decrease, notably in terms of long-term capital, since there is less need to immobilize funds for several years.

Furthermore, in terms of cash flow, there is a payment interval favorable to the company using it, as in this type of organization of production, the service is paid for once it has been provided, i.e. later than in a classic activity.

Recourse to Laborgistics® is thus particularly valuable in financial terms, since in addition to the flexibility and rapid response that this type of production organization affords, it obviates the need to call on long-term capital, is favorable to cash flow and therefore entails fewer financial risks.

Generally speaking, Laborgistics® transfers part of the financial cost onto the service provider called upon.

With respect to staffing, Laborgistics® modifies the scale and mode of organization of staffing within companies. The purpose of the human resources function, as seen above, is the day-to-day management of employees alongside human and social development.

By calling upon external service providers, it is clear that Laborgistics® will have an influence on the number of salaried employees within the company. By retaining only those employees necessary to the functioning of the core business, it becomes natural to cut jobs, to reclassify or to retrain within the principal company.

Most of the time, the salaried employees who are kept on after the implementation of Laborgistics® are specialists. Managing them is not the same as managing a more heterogeneous body of workers, as their expectations, motivations, development and remuneration are quite specific. Finally, the mental preparation of all the staff before any implementation of Laborgistics® is often decisive for its successful completion.

A new body of specialists must also be constituted to monitor the work of outside service providers. It will be made up of qualified personnel with confirmed technical skills, a global vision of the production process and sound legal knowledge. This unit will be separate from the purchasing department, which, unlike the case of simple subcontracting, cannot act alone in monitoring the Laborgistics®

process. Occasionally, it may be necessary to set up a steering committee bringing together the principal and the external service provider, not only to monitor Laborgistics® operations but also to modify Laborgistics® contracts in the event of a change in circumstances.

Ultimately, the department set up internally to monitor the outside providers will have to be able to "have things done" rather than acting itself in the traditional manner. It will be assessed on its capacity to manage a long-term contract rather than merely on its technical skills. To do so, it will be necessary to call upon experienced individuals capable of assessing the implications of Laborgistics® at a company-wide level.

In terms of production, i.e. everything bearing on the organization and running of operations, from ensuring the availability of required materials to delivering the finished product to the customer, Laborgistics® clearly has a role of paramount importance.

More and more frequently, competitive pressure leads to production being organized on a tight-flow or "just-in-time" basis, ensuring that the intended quantities of components or products are delivered to the right place at the right time. Such a system is designed for two concurrent purposes: to reduce the response time of the production system to the quantitative and qualitative fluctuations in demand and to eliminate wasteful practices.

Improving response time means reducing the duration of the production life cycle, which itself means reducing stocks at all levels: raw materials, interim stocks and finished products. Suppliers are obliged to deliver more rapidly and more frequently, and the circulation among sites of products being manufactured must be speeded up. In this respect, reducing stocks is not an end, but simply a means.

A tight-flow system requires flexible organization of production, so that it may be adapted rapidly to quantitative and more especially qualitative changes in demand. However, at the same time, it means profound change in many behavior patterns. The most visible aspect is the relationship between the suppliers and outside service providers with regard to the supplies required by the company.

It is of course in this context that Laborgistics® plays an essential role in ensuring greater flexibility, thus enabling the production system to reach its objectives in terms of both quantity and quality.

With regard to the marketing function, Laborgistics® makes it possible to improve the functioning of relations between the company and its clients. While it is difficult to define marketing accurately, it is possible to say that the function is based on two general principles:

– The constant preoccupation with adapting production to consumer potential, meaning that all producers must study the market whenever a decision has to be made.

– The average consumer does not exist, and each buyer has specific needs and behavior patterns. All companies must therefore divide the market into groups of consumers having more or less the same aspirations, i.e. they must segment the market into homogeneous subsets.

This is why a product, in marketing terms, is defined by three component parts: its form, its use (i.e. the need it satisfies) and its users (i.e. the customer base for which it has been designed).

Until the end of the First World War, the major preoccupation was to produce rather than to sell. In such a context, marketing was reduced to its simplest form, and was limited to the auxiliary activity of distributing the products. At that time, it was more difficult to produce than to sell goods and services.

In less than half a century, in all developed countries, this conception changed considerably. With the proliferation of companies and available products, the seller's market has become a buyer's market, in which the customer base has become a decisive factor.

Through the flexibility it brings to production systems, Laborgistics® makes it possible to adapt production constantly to the needs and expectations of the consumers, who have become particularly demanding.

Furthermore, it should be added that through Laborgistics®, certain fixed costs are transformed into variable costs, the average cost of a product falls and the incremental costs rise. This new development makes it possible to determine prices much closer to the expectations of the consumers.

Parallel to this, an increasing need for information and communication technologies has appeared with the recourse to the market inherent in a Laborgistics®-based approach. The role of ICTs has been expanding constantly over the past few years. Within companies, as Laborgistics® has developed, the simple need for information consisting in bringing together people and events has turned into a need for communication, i.e. an exchange of information among individuals, notably suppliers, outside service providers and of course clients, whatever their geographical location may be.

For accounting, Laborgistics® gives rise to a number of effects, notably in the field of cost accounting. Cost accounting has the following objectives:

– Diagnosis: Does the market price allow for a margin? What should be done to lower costs?

– Decision-making: Should the production process be modified? Should Laborgistics® be applied? Should production be halted?

– Monitoring: Are the rises in expenditure too great?

Since Laborgistics® lowers fixed costs, cost accounting is thus much easier to set up. More specifically, increased awareness of the direct costs means that the calculation of the cost price is simpler and more accurate.

Furthermore, as Laborgistics® contracts are carried out over several years, it is more convenient to calculate the forecast cost price, since the duration of the contract limits the risks that may arise from fluctuations in cost due to new developments in the environment.

With regard to general management, Laborgistics® influences the strategies of companies. The process of developing strategy under the aegis of the general management is based on a comparison of the firm's objectives, its competencies and the characteristics of its environment. These factors are in a situation of dynamic interdependence, in that they evolve both autonomously and under the influence of the others. Furthermore, each of them is sensitive to the actions of agencies both internal and external to the firm, the information and behavior of which partly depend on the structures in which they operate.

The decision to refocus on the core business and to use Laborgistics® to run a certain number of operations calls into question corporate strategies in response to market expectations in an increasingly competitive environment. This is why the decision can only be made by the CEO rather than directors of technical departments, although the latter may be of assistance on certain specific questions.

Laborgistics® thus impacts all the functions of the company, and this new phenomenon, according to Rifkin[1], should continue to expand. In his view, this mode of organization, leading to what he terms "hollow companies", should become the norm. There is currently a school of thought that considers that the source of compet-

---

1. J. Rifkin, *The Age of Access*, Putman, 2001.

itive edge no longer lies in fixed assets such as machines and buildings, but in "abstract" assets such as trademarks, know-how and patents. By ridding themselves of activities that consume a great deal of physical capital, these hollow companies are able to concentrate their strategy on the enhancement of intangible elements. For Rifkin, the enhanced stock market value of Coca-Cola reflects the price that the financial markets give to this world-famous brand, which is far higher than the value of its factories. Furthermore, Coca-Cola has its products made by external service providers based where the markets are.

Macroeconomic Influences

Through its efforts to obtain flexibility, rapid response and lower costs, Laborgistics® leads, as seen above, to modifying a country's production system. At the same time, the abolition of trade barriers and increasingly widespread competition among countries encourage companies to relocate certain activities to countries with lower cost structures.

The Goldman Sachs investment bank will be transferring six million jobs in the service sector from the United States over the next few years, and according to Forbes Magazine, 400 of the thousand largest companies are announcing their intention to relocate their service activities. A similar process can be observed in Europe.

The global economy has now entered a sort of global mobility revolution. While the service companies themselves are not relocating, a large number of the tasks they have performed up to now have been transferred. These transfers occur from north to south – from Europe or the United States to India or Mexico – but south-to-south movements can also be observed, for example from Bangladesh to China. In short, the entire tertiary sector is relocating. A new union, United Network International (UNI), has even been set up to fill the need for social dialog across borders, and this union now has 15 million members in 150 countries.

All over the world, these new relationships among countries have had a positive impact, contrary to what is often heard.

To measure the effects of this liberalization of the economy, the World Bank sets the level of absolute poverty at $1 per person per day. From 1990 to 1999 (latest statistics available) the percentage of persons living in such conditions fell from 29.6% to 23.2%. Naturally, the statistics vary greatly from one continent to another.

India: the World's Office

In the space of ten years, India has become the world center for IT service outsourcing. Initially, this concerned only simple tasks such as staffing call centers or inputting data. Today, the focus is on research and development for General Electric, Google, SNECMA and Intel, to name but a few. According to Nasscom (the National Association of Software and Service Companies) there are now 200,000 people in India working in export-oriented services. In McKinsey's view, this figure will have risen to 4 million by 2008.

China's situation has greatly improved and Latin America's has remained stable, while living conditions have deteriorated in the former Soviet bloc. According to J.M. Severino[1], "globalization is a long-term phenomenon, the perspectives of which have changed and will continue to change in the future". He considers that in the space of half a century, striking improvements have been made to the living conditions of the world's population.

In the developing countries, life expectancy has risen by over 20 years, from 41 to 64, and the population having access to drinking water has risen from 35% to 80% today. Infant mortality has fallen by half, and revenue has increased by 250% since 1965 outside the rich countries.

Severino has also stated that to attain a middle-class standard of living, an income of some USD 6,000 a year is needed. This is the case for 290 million Chinese, 90 million Indians and 60 million Brazilians, but there are still very poor countries like Pakistan and Nigeria where the middle class accounts for less than 5% of the population.

This emergence of a middle class is essential, for not only does it make it possible to develop consumption but also it is indispensable for financing investments.

It may be concluded that while globalization does favor certain regions, on the whole it is nevertheless a positive trend.

While China is in the process of becoming "the world's factory", in a few years, India may well be "the world's office".

---

1. Director of the French Development Agency and former Vice-President of the World Bank

---

Success Story

After three years of existence, the largest IT subcontracting company in India (Business Process Outsourcing) boasts over 8,400 staff. The average age of employees is 23, and their salaries range from EUR 1,500 to 1,800 a year.

Today, IT subcontracting in India employs 170,000 people. But by 2008, this number will have risen to almost a million, carrying out not only the repetitive tasks they do today but implementing Laborgistics®, "with significant creation of added value", in the words of Raman Roy, the founder of Business Process Outsourcing.

Laborgistics® thus fulfills a need for organizations wishing to become more flexible, to respond more rapidly and to be more efficient. However, recourse to the market is part of an environment tending towards liberalization. While strengthening companies in the industrialized countries, the poorest countries are able to obtain considerable advantages, which in turn will enable them to achieve growth and development ultimately having a positive impact on the whole population. Globalization and Laborgistics® together thus make it possible to reduce poverty. This is why, in Trainar's view, the protection of the freedom to found companies and to set up exchanges, along with the protection of foreign investments, is an essential factor in development policy.

GLOSSARY OF TERMS & CONCEPTS

CONCURRENT ENGINEERING

Concurrent engineering is a management method which involves carrying out a project by involving all relevant staff concurrently including the suppliers, right from the beginning of the design rather than sequentially, as is usually the case. Thus, in classic management models, the product is first designed, then developed and lastly, the marketing plans are prepared. With this new technique honed in Japan, it is possible to perfect the products by carrying out the tasks simultaneously and thus launch them earlier. This method has been proved effective: having studied 29 development programs for cars between 1963 and 1987, a Harvard Business School professor showed that Japanese cars required an average of 46 months of technical research as opposed to 60 months in the US.

Swift access to the market is a key factor for success in a competitive environment and requires transverse vision of the various functions involved in project development. Concurrent engineering is based on the setting up of an outline simultaneously encompassing the design of the project and its organization. It is then capable of incorporating, in real time, a wealth of complex and diverse information relative to the shape and manufacturing of the product and to fold in the necessary administrative and organizational procedures. For this it is necessary to create database systems capable of processing the information required to carry out all the stages involved in the project. This is a decision-making process that recurs in Laborgistics®.

CORE COMPETENCIES

Core business or key competencies are terms specifying all the skills and technologies required by a firm to offer a real, long-lasting added value to customers, whatever the changes may occur on the market.

Core competencies are often held by a very small number of firms at a given moment and they are not necessarily limited and narrow. The Japanese firm Honda, for example, started out with a recognized competency in spark ignition engines, they then went on to manufacture motorbikes, cars and lawnmowers etc. For G. Hamel and C.K. Prahalad[1], who coined the term, core competency must be able to answer the following three questions:
– Does it allow for potential access to a wide variety of markets?
– Can it provide a real contribution to consumer expectations?
– Is it difficult for competitors to imitate?

Core competencies represent what the theory of institutional economics terms "dynamic capacities" or "specific assets". They require considerable investment to maintain a competitive edge, even while changes in the environment may call into question these acquired skills and transform them into extra outlay for the firm. The refocusing on core competencies leads to the setting up of new working methods, especially encouraging the out-sourcing of a certain number of functions to other firms on the market, and as such, it is an approach that encourages the development of Laborgistics®.

DELAYERING

Delayering calls into question the traditional hierarchical organization. This management method is based on a flatter structure, achieved by reducing the number of hierarchical levels within the firm. It thus makes for swifter decision-making, shorter communication circuits, greater stimulation and broad employee participation in the management of the firm.

Firms which opt for delayering automatically cut costs. For some, cost-cutting is the primary aim of restructuring. For others, a flatter organization is above all the means to eliminate cumbersome red tape, to achieve swifter communication and the development of a customer-oriented corporate culture within which teamwork and working methods are based on more active employee participation.

---

1. Their article "The Core Competence of the Corporation", *Harvard Business Review*, May-June 1990, received the McKinsey award.

This type of organization may be set up in various ways, first, by eliminating or automating certain management activities, then by pinpointing and re-allocating costs that are too high or do not serve any purpose. Delayering in fact means streamlining and in-depth modification of the role of the hierarchy (see also flat organization).

DOWNSIZING

While, from 1950 to 1980, the watchword among managers was "big is beautiful", this idea has since been called into question. The unchecked growth in the size of firms is no longer necessarily at the root of productivity or an increase in profits. Thus, when British Telecom was privatized in 1984, its sales were around 11 billion dollars, its profits 2 billion and the number of its employees close on 250,000. Ten years later, this telecom firm had shed 100,000 employees but its sales had doubled and its profits were three times as high.

Downsizing is not a mere reduction in staff levels to generate lower charges, it is rather reengineering (see this word) which leads to the overhaul of the firm's entire strategy with, naturally, a decrease in staff levels, alongside more aggressive marketing, new investments and partnerships which not only lead to a reduction in costs but encourage innovative solutions.

At the beginning of the 1980s, downsizing programs were shown to be ill tailored to improving corporate situations, since managers had been trained to look to the firm's growth as the sole criterion for performance (upsizing). Consequently, those employees who were made redundant felt that they had been betrayed by management and those remained in the firm after downsizing, felt demoralized. This is why, for this type of reorganization to be successful, the way must be paved and people must be prepared psychologically *via* intense communication for all personnel. In fact, the aim of downsizing is to eliminate red tape by making firms leaner in order to increase their competitive edge.

EMPOWERMENT

Empowerment is a term coined by Rosabeth Moss Kanter, a Harvard Business School professor. This method consists in granting employees a greater degree of autonomy and more responsibilities. Authority is thus shared out differently at all levels. This method is based on information transmission circuits, for "information is power". Naturally, this new distribution of authority has largely

benefited from the development of new information and communication technologies. Managers are thus becoming partners rather
than bosses. Thus, employees each assume their responsibilities,
take the decisions appropriate to their level and are assessed in the
light of their own results.

In practical terms, empowerment leads either to greater autonomy in the execution of tasks, or to the forming of self-reliant
teams. Delegating responsibility here is considered necessarily as
contributing to motivation. However, this transformation of power
circuits can have perverse impact if, for example, certain employees
refuse to play the game or if it leads to a great number of meetings
in which nothing is decided. Consequently, this method must not
lead to the total elimination of management and, if it is to be effective, must comprise a change in the assessment and reward system.

FLAT ORGANIZATION

The aim of this type of organization is to restrict the levels of
management as much as possible in order to eliminate the intermediaries and thus avoid the multiplication of superfluous communication (this process being known as delayering).

In traditional, hierarchical organizations, authority works one-
way (top to bottom) and is only rarely delegated, whereas in flat
organizations, it can take many different directions and forms
according to the tasks or projects to be carried out. The key notion
is that the employees, working individually or in teams and enjoy-
ing a high degree of latitude to reach their objectives, are more productive than employees who are supervised too closely. An organization of this type is mostly possible only in small firms having
adopted a traditional hierarchy. For large organizations, power
cannot be entirely delegated and hierarchy done away with, managers are needed to hone policy, monitor work and ensure that all the
employees comply with the aims that have been set.

FLEXIBLE ORGANIZATION

Over the past years, the word flexible has become a managers'
favorite. Systems of production, working hours and organizations
must nowadays be flexible. Flexibility is sought in order to respond
swiftly to market developments and bring about change in management. Laborgistics® is a method of business organization that provides a response to this requirement in firms of today.

HORIZONTAL CORPORATION

Horizontal organization is a form of organization that is replacing traditional, vertical, pyramid hierarchy. It is a constantly-changing type of structure. The end aim is customer satisfaction, achieved by organizing the firm around various processes rather than mere tasks, with few hierarchical levels.

Seven elements characterize this type of organization, as noted by Business Week in 1993 in "The Horizontal Corporation":

– a firm working around a small number of key processes rather than functions or departments;

– restricted hierarchy to eliminate superfluous work;

– teams are given a free rein, provided they follow management directives;

– customers can choose their own method to evaluate performance;

– a system is set up to reward all employees rather than individuals;

– forging of customer and supplier relations rooted in trust rather than only on contracts;

– putting together a training and information pack for all employees.

JUST IN TIME

The underlying notion of Just In Time (JIT) consists in producing and delivering goods, avoiding both surpluses and shortages. This notion rapidly became a key element in Japanese quality control.

Credit for the creation and honing of Just in Time goes to Taiichi Ohno, a Toyota manager. Later, he suggested generalizing this approach to the entire industry using a communication instrument, kanban, which means etiquette in Japanese. It is a kind of quality control indicator for upstream workshops to adapt their production to match demand from downstream workshops. The kanban circulates between workshops and comes back to the beginning of the manufacturing process at the end of each cycle, thus making it possible to avoid waste and eliminate all surplus. The kanban system, also known as the "zero stock" or "Just In Time" method, is actually an integrated organization of production, stock and quality. It is thus a far cry from the traditional, hierarchical firms based on centralized coordination of the various functions.

LABORGISTICS®

Laborgistics® is a term coined by a Franco-American firm, International Outsourcing Services (IOS), which means literally: service activity based on work that is organized and executed logically.

This form of business organization fits into the scheme of Concurrent Engineering which consists in getting all partners involved in future manufacturing operations, right from the outset with product design. Laborgistics® is close to what is known as "contract manufacturing" in which some production is no longer considered to be core business and must be entrusted to other firms specializing in this sphere.

This is the most elaborate form of outsourcing and is necessarily part of a long-term corporate vision in which the constraints linked to production have to be as flexible as possible in order to innovate and improve performance.

LEAN COMPANY

For J. Brilman, the lean company is "a firm which has set up Total Quality Management (TQM), Just in Time (JIT) and Concurrent Engineering and all that results with respect to organization and working methods".

This organization which aims to increase productivity and product quality fits into the notions known as "Toyotism" as practiced by automaker Toyota. This new form of organization contrasts with Fordism based on integrated mass production. This new corporate design consists in both breaking production down into small units to set up flexible management and outsourcing as much as possible.

For certain experts, this type of organization sparked what has been termed "the Japanese Miracle", even if the Japanese no longer hold the monopoly, given that most US automakers have also applied it.

LEARNING ORGANIZATION

The Learning firm[1] is an organization in which the individual and joint learning process is constant and ongoing, in order to improve the competencies and knowledge of its members.

It is based on men and women who have learnt how to learn, can adapt, have an inquiring mind, are interested in a host of subjects and make personal investments in the firm's future. It is also an

---

1. This term was coined by P. Senge in *The Fifth Discipline*, published by Bantam Doubleday Day in 1990.

organization that focuses firmly on innovation, is open to outside influence and which strives to avoid conservative reflexes.

The learning organization, according to P. Senge, is based on five major elements:

- systems thinking;
- personal mastery;
- mental models;
- building shared vision;
- team learning.

This organization implies being open to outside influence and having personnel capable of grasping all the interrelations between activities and staff and who, as a team, are constantly striving to learn to become an "intelligent firm"[1].

REENGINEERING

Reengineering posits that most processes do not function as well as they should and that it is crucial to carry out swift transformations.

M. Hammer and J. Champy[2], who coined this term, consider that change is not expressed in terms of strategy or marketing but according to a single watchword "get on your bike, roll your sleeves up and get moving".

The following principles are characteristic of reengineering:

- rolling several professions into one;
- letting employees make decisions;
- following a natural order to carry out each stage in the process;
- recognizing that there are many versions of each process;
- carrying out work in a consistent manner;
- cutting down on downtime and monitoring;
- doing the work first and the report after;
- encouraging decentralized initiatives.

In fact, reengineering is a response to waste and productivity crises within major organizations as observed in the 1990s, which furthermore explains its runaway success. US automakers especially have had recourse to this and it has saved them millions of dollars and thousands of jobs.

---

1. A concept developed by J. B. Quinn, management professor at Dartmouth College, thrice winner of the McKinsey Award for best article published by the Harvard Business School.

2. *Op. cit.*

SHAMROCK ORGANIZATION

Credit for the term "shamrock organization" goes to British writer C. Handy[1].

It is a process-based type of organization, which replaces the traditional hierarchical pyramid.

A small central group of managers represents the heart of the shamrock, reflecting the core competencies of the firm, i.e. its strategic resources and the specific competencies on which the firm is based. It is in this centre that operations and the plan of action are coordinated. As for the three leaves linked to the centre, but not to each other, they represent: the core business or full-time work unit, outsourced B2B relations or the people or firms with which contracts are drawn up to carry out all non-essential tasks and lastly the contingency workforce or part-time employees, seasonal workers and professionals with specific skills who are called upon as necessary. The logics of shamrock organization are to keep permanent staff to a minimum for a high level of effectiveness, cutting down drastically on other staff and costs and out-sourcing as much as possible, even if this kind of refocusing is not always well-received among the employees whose jobs are being shelved.

VIRTUAL CORPORATION

A virtual product is a product which may be available at any time, in any place and in any variety. According to W. Davidow and M. Malone[2], the authors of a major work on the subject, a virtual firm is defined as an organization the structure of which is based on alliances with partners and suppliers and having recourse to a vast network of service providers to supply standard goods and services and thus meet consumer demand.

An organization of this type employs a small group of workers focusing on strategic priorities and who trade physically with other firms. The Virtual Corporation is founded on the following key elements:

– time, considered a key element in access to the market;
– trust-based supplier relations;
– rapidity and flexibility of operations as an organizational force.

---

1. *The Age of Unreason*, Harvard Business School Press, 1990.
2. *Op. Cit.*

Telecommunication networks and new information and communication technologies are crucial factors for the development of this type of organization. In general, virtual firms translate into a variety of organizational options combining flexibility, responsiveness, low costs and top-quality service.

APPENDIX 1

Outsourcing Charter

To ensure outsourcing success, the MEDEF (French Business Confederation) has suggested adhering to a certain number of principles in the form of a "charter" that may be borne in mind for Laborgistics®.

1. Outsourcing is a strategic issue.
2. Outsourcing supposes a legally binding commitment that's clear and well-balanced.
3. Outsourcing is people-oriented.
4. Outsourcing requires a shared culture.

Source : Club Esprit Service.

APPENDIX 2

To Do it, or to Have it Done

Top 10 Reasons Companies Outsource

1. Reduce and control operating costs
2. Improve company focus
3. Gain access to world-class capabilities
4. Free internal resources for other purposes
5. Resources are not available internally
6. Accelerate reengineering benefits
7. Function difficult to manage/Out of control
8. Make capital funds available
9. Share risks
10. Cash infusion

Top 10 Factors for Successful Outsourcing

1. Understands company goals and objectives
2. A strategic vision and plan
3. Selecting the right vendor
4. Ongoing management of the relationships
5. A properly structured contract
6. Open communications with affected individual/groups
7. Senior excutive supports and involvement
8. Careful attention to personel issues
9. Near term financial justification
10. Use of outside expertise

Top 10 Factors in Vendor Selection

1. Commitment to quality
2. Price
3. References/reputations
4. Flexible contract terms
5. Scope of ressources
6. Additional value – added capability
7. Cultural match
8. Existing relationship
9. Location
10. Other

Source : Survey of Currents and Potential Outsourcing End-Users
The Outsourcing Institute, 1998.

BIBLIOGRAPHY

Ansoff H. and Brandebourg R., August 1971, A Language for Organization Design, *Management Science.*

Clausewitz K. von, 1832, *On War.*

Coase R., 1937, The Nature of the Firm, *Economica*, vol. 4.

Dawidow W. and Malone M., 1993, The Virtual Corporation, *Business Week.*

Drucker F., 1954, *The Practice of Management*, New York, Harper.

Drucker F., 2003, *Managing in The Next Society*, Treeman Talley Books.

Ernst and Young, 2003, *Baromètre de l'outsourcing, pratiques et tendances de l'externalisation en France (Outsourcing Barometer, outsourcing practices and trends in France).*

Fayol H., 1916, *Administration industrielle et générale (General and Industrial Management)*, reissue. 1979, Paris, Dunod.

Gerstner L., 2002, *Who Says Elephants Can't Dance?* Harper-Business.

Guillaume M. and Roux D., 1999, L'économie hi-tech (The Hi-tech Economy), in *Espérances et menaces de l'an 2000 (Hopes and Threats in 2000)*, Paris, Descartes & Cie.

Hamel G. and Prahalad C., 1990, *The Core Competence of the Corporation*, Harvard Business Review, n° 68.

Hammer M. and Champy J., 1993, *Reengineering the Corporation: a Manifesto for Business Revolution*, Harper Collins Publishers, New York.

Handy C., 1990, *The Age of Unreason*, Harvard Business School Press.

Hicks J., 1969, *A Theory of Economic History*, Oxford, Clarence Press.

Jarillo J.C., 1988, On Strategic Networks, *Strategic Management Journal*.

Lacity M. and Hirschheim R., 1993, *The Information Systems Outsourcing Bandwagon*, Sloan Management Review, 13-25.

Lei D. and Hitt M., 1995, 21, 5, 835-859, Strategic Restructuring and Outsourcing: the Effects of Mergers and Acquisitions and LBOs on Building Firm Skills and Capabilities, *Journal of Management*.

Novamétrie and Microsoft, Sep. 2003, Réflexions stratégiques sur la transformation des entreprises (Strategic Reflections on Corporate Transformation), *The Observatory of Chairmen and CEOs*, Novamétrie and Microsoft.

Pascale R.T., 1990, *Managing on the Edge*, The Free Press.

Patry M., 2000, *Faire ou faire faire : la prospective de l'économie des organisations (To Do it, or to Have it Done: the Future of Organization Economy)*, CIRANO-HEC, Montréal.

Porter M., 1980, *Competitive Strategy: Techniques for Analyzing Industries and Competitors*, New York The Free Press.

Porter M., 1985, *Competitive Advantage*, New York, The Free Press

Porter M. and Millar V., July 1985, How information gives you competitive advantage, *Harvard Business Review*.

Quinn J.B., 1992, *The Intelligent Enterprise: a Knowledge and Service-Based Paradigm for the Industry*, New York, The Free Press.

Quinn J. and Hilmer F., Summer 1994, Strategic Outsourcing, *Sloan Management Review*.

Rifkin J., 2001, *The Age of Access: The New Culture of Hypercapitalism*, Putman.

Simon H., 1960, *The New Science of Management Decision*, New York, Harper & Row.

Taylor F.W., 1911, *The Principles of Scientific Management*.

Taylor F.W., 1903, *Shop Management*.

Thomas L.G., 1996, *Organization Science*.

Thorelli H.B., 1986, Networks: Between Markets and Hierarchies, *Strategic Management Journal vol. 7*.

Williamson O.E., 1975, *Market and Hierarchies*, Free Press, New York.

Williamson O.E., 1985, *The Economic Institutions of Capitalism*, Free Press, New York. Williamson O.E., 1993, Strategizing, Economizing, and Economic Organization, *Strategic Management Journal*.

INDEX

Réalisé en P.A.O. par STDI - Z. A. Route de Couterne - 53110 Lassay-les-Châteaux
N° 358111X - *Imprimé en France.* - JOUVE, 11, bd de Sébastopol, 75001 PARIS